RAISING TEENAGERS
TO CHOOSE WISELY

Methods for Raising Well-behaved and Intelligent Children

Bukky Ekine-Ogunlana

© Copyright Bukky Ekine-Ogunlana 2025 – All rights reserved.

The content contained within this book may not be reproduced, duplicated, or transmitted without direct written permission from the author or the publisher.

Under no circumstance should any blame or legal responsibility be held against the publisher, or author, for any damages, reparation, or monetary loss due to the information contained within this book. Either directly or indirectly. You are responsible for your own choices, actions, and results.

Legal Notice:

This book is copyright protected. This book is only for personal use. You cannot amend, distribute, sell, use, quote, or paraphrase any part, or the content within this book, without the consent of the author or publisher.

Disclaimer Notice:

Please note the information contained within this document is for educational and entertainment purposes only. All effort has been executed to present accurate, up-to-date, and reliable, complete information. No warranties of any kind are declared or implied. Readers acknowledge that the author is not engaging in the rendering of legal, financial, medical, or professional advice. The content within this book has been derived from various sources. Please consult a licensed professional before attempting any techniques outlined in this book

By reading this document, the reader agrees that under no circumstances is the author responsible for any losses, direct or indirect, which are incurred as a result of the use of the information contained within this document, including, but not limited to,—errors, omissions, or inaccuracies.

Published by

TCEC Publishing

TCEC House

England, Great Britain

Dedication

This book is dedicated to our three amazing children and all the beautiful children worldwide who have passed through the T.C.E.C 6-16 years program over the years. Thank you for the opportunity to serve you and invest in your colorful and bright future.

Table of Content

Introduction: Raising Teens in a Loud, Big World And Keeping Them Secure 7

Chapter 1: The Power of Choice Helping Your Teen Choose Life 13

Chapter 2: Building a Foundation of Trust Creating Safety for Honest Conversations 21

Chapter 3: Instilling Godly Values Building a Compass for Life 32

Chapter 4: Helping Your Teen Stand Tall in a World That Pulls Them Down 41

Chapter 5: Why Wisdom Matters Teaching Your Teen to Choose Wisely 48

Chapter 6: Anchoring Your Teen's Heart in Godly Wisdom . 54

Chapter 7: Raising Deliverers Preparing Teens to Choose Wisely in a Dark World 64

Chapter 8: "Proverbs in Real Life: Stories to Inspire and Guide Teens 79

Chapter 9: Taming Technology Without Losing Your Sanity (or Your Teen) 113

Chapter 10: Overcoming Challenges Together Walking Through Storms as a Family 120

Father's Teachings 131

Conclusion: Raising Teens with a Legacy of Wisdom 160

Please Leave a Review! 163

Other Books You'll Love! 164

Your Free Gift! 169

References 170

Introduction
Raising Teens in a Loud, Big World
And Keeping Them Secure

If you're holding this book right now, you're probably in the thick of it right now—the loud, messy, and beautiful chaos that comes with parenting a teenager.

Let's take a moment to be very honest: it's not always easy. Sometimes it feels like a rollercoaster. One minute, everything is going on well and fine with your teen is talking to you, sharing a moment, maybe even laughing. And the next minute? There's a slammed door, a silence that stretches across the room, and a knot in your stomach that won't go away.

I know a mom who told me about a night when her son slammed his bedroom door so hard that it shook the entire house. She stood there, her heart racing, wondering if she had said the wrong thing. *Had she lost him?* Or worse, *had she completely messed this up?* The silence in the house was deafening. The kind that made her ask silent questions, *How do I reach him, what do I need to do, How do I go about it? What if I've failed as a parent?*

If you've ever found yourself standing outside a door, wondering what happened to the close connection you used to have, know that you're not alone in this as you are wondering. Many parents, like you, are navigating the turbulent waters of parenting a teenager, and we're here to support and understand you.

Parenting a teenager can feel like trying to steer a tiny boat in a vast, stormy ocean. Some days the waters are nice and really calm, and you feel like you're making progress. Other days, you get hit by waves of hormones, peer pressure, social media chaos, cultural confusion, slammed doors, and those painful, quiet dinners where no one says a word.

You start asking yourself:
- *Am I saying the right things?*
- *Do they even hear me?*
- *What happens when I'm not around to guide them?*

There are those **2 a.m. moments** filled with doubt, worry, overthinking, and plenty of failures. But here's what I've learned through it all: you don't have to be a perfect parent. You need to be a present one.

Even if your teen doesn't say it outright, deep down, they long for your steady presence. The kind of love that says, *I'm here for you, no matter what.* They need you to believe in them, even when they don't believe in themselves. They need your guidance, even when they push it away. And they need to know you think they can become wise, strong, and faith-filled adults—especially when the world around them is telling them otherwise.

A Story of Small Moments Making a Big Difference

Let's rewind a bit to a chilly Thursday night. A mother and her teenage daughter sat at the kitchen table, both exhausted from the day's activities. And suddenly, out of nowhere, her daughter whispered, *"I'm scared about school... and everything else."* Her voice cracked as if holding back years of bottled-up fears which she had.

Instead of jumping in with advice to give her or trying to "fix it," this mom just listened. She didn't try to solve anything. They discussed the pressure together—expectations from friends, school, and within themselves.

Then, she shared something she had learned in her own life: *"Faith doesn't mean you're never afraid. It means you trust God for whom He is and what He has promised, even when fear is very loud."*

Something shifted that night. Her daughter felt seen. She didn't feel alone anymore. Later, when she curled up in bed, her mom quietly prayed—asking God to continue opening her heart to His quiet, steady voice amidst the noise of life.

That's what builds security in teens: not big speeches or perfect solutions, but the small, sacred moments of presence, listening, and prayer. These moments, though seemingly insignificant, have the power to transform and inspire, giving hope even amid chaos.

This Book is Part of a Bigger Journey

This book won't hand you a magic formula, no, it will not. But it will walk with you through the ups and downs that you can relate with, the slammed doors, and the quiet victories. It will provide you with tools to help build a relationship where your teen feels safe enough to make wise decisions, even when the world around them feels loud and chaotic.

- **Part One – Parenting Teenage Boys for Purpose** focuses on helping young men discover who they are, how they're wired, and what they're called to do.

- **Part Two – Parenting Teenage Girls for Purpose** explores how to cultivate confidence, discernment, and a deep-rooted faith in young women who are pulled in countless directions.

And this third part—the one you're holding—brings it all together. It's about creating a home where teens feel secure enough to make godly choices, even when the world is trying to pull them off track.

The Hard Truth: Life Requires Sacrifice

Jesus said, *"Unless a grain of wheat falls into the earth and dies, it remains alone; but if it dies, it bears much fruit."* (John 12:24) Parenting teens is full of these small "deaths"—moments where we let go of convenience, control, or even our comfort, all for their sake.

One parent shared how she stayed up late, helping her son prepare for a nerve-wracking school presentation. It was the last thing she wanted to do after a long day as she was tired and just wanted to sleep but she did not. The son was grumpy, tired, and showed little gratitude. But years later, he thanked her—for showing up, for believing in him when he didn't believe in himself. **These are the moments that bear fruit.**

Why Raising Teens Wisely Matters

The teenage years can feel like a rollercoaster ride, filled with so many questions about identity, purpose, and where they belong in the world. As a parent, your job isn't just to survive these years—it's to help your teen thrive. To guide them with purpose, wisdom, and grounded faith which are the essentials.

This book is here to assist you:

- **Connect deeply with your teen, beyond surface-level struggles that is obvious.**

- **Lean into spiritual truths that bring clarity when the world feels confusing**

- **Empower your teen to live wisely and courageously, even when the world doesn't**

Practical Ways to Start Today

You don't have to wait for the "perfect" moment. Here are some simple ways to get started:

- **Create space for honest and real conversations**: Maybe it's during a quiet car ride or after the dinner. Ask, "What's been on your mind lately?" or "What's been the hardest part of this week for you?"

- **Listen more than you speak**: You don't have to fix it all. Sometimes, just being there and listening gives you insight into the unspoken words and this is the best thing you can do.

- **Please share your struggles**: Let your teen know they're not the only one who feels lost or overwhelmed sometimes.

- **Pray together**: Even a simple prayer can plant lasting seeds of faith.

- **Notice the small moments**: When your teen pauses to make a decision, or they sense something more profound stirring within—that's often God whispering. Don't miss those moments.

Parenting teens isn't easy. It's messy, humbling, and full of unknowns. But with faith, presence, and open hearts, you can build a safe harbor—where your teenager feels seen, supported, and secure enough to become exactly who God made them to be.

After reading this book, I'd be grateful if you could leave a quick review. Even a few sentences would mean the world to me! Thank you for being part of this journey."

Chapter 1
The Power of Choice
Helping Your Teen Choose Life

*"See, I have set before you today life and good, death and evil... therefore choose life, that you and your offspring may live." — **Deuteronomy 30:15,19***

Any parent who has watched their teenager walk out the door—backpack slung over one shoulder, phone in hand, earbuds in—knows the feeling: that quiet knot in the stomach. The silent, hopeful prayer: *Please, let them make good choices today.*

That realization—that you can't control everything—often comes sooner than expected. One mother remembers when her son was just twelve. His friends dared him to sneak a video game into the house behind her back. And he did. The truth came out, of course—because secrets rarely stay hidden for long.

That moment sent her into a quiet panic: *If he's pushing boundaries now, what happens when it's about dating, driving, drinking, or deep faith decisions when I'm not around?*

The truth is, teens face crossroads every single day—decisions about:

- Friendships
- Identity
- Boundaries
- Who or what they allow to shape their heart and mind

And here's the hard truth: you won't always be there to intervene. You can't intercept every moment of temptation or peer pressure that comes to them. And that thought? It's really terrifying.

But this is where God's design becomes clear. Parenting teens isn't about controlling every outcome. It's about helping them to exercise their will, to understand the **power of their own choice**—a divine gift that carries weight, purpose, and responsibility.

Why God Gave Us a Choice:
Why God Gave Us a Choice: The Robot and the Best Friend

Imagine you're a brilliant inventor. You build a robot—one that's programmed to clean your home, compliment you, follow every command, and say, "I love you" every time you walk in the room.

At first, it seems perfect does it not?

But after a while, those words start to feel empty. Why?

Because the robot **has no choice**. It says "I love you" because it was built to—not because it means it.

Now imagine your **teenager**—messy room, strong opinions, mood swings and all. They're not programmed. They have their own will. They can choose to obey or disobey, to pull away or lean in.

So when that teen looks you in the eye and says, "I love you"—**you know it's real**. Because they didn't have to say it. They chose to.

Real love only matters when it's a choice.

Take it one step further.

Imagine you're going through a hard time, and your **best friend** shows up. Not because you called, not because they had to—but because they chose to.

They listened. Sat with you. Prayed for you.

That kind of love means something—**because it wasn't forced.**

It was **free. Intentional. Genuine.**

This Is Why God Gave Us Free Will

God could have created robots to worship Him.

He could've programmed us to follow every rule without question.

But that wouldn't be love. That would be **control**.

True love must be chosen.

That's why God gave Adam and Eve the option to say no—because without choice, love isn't real.

God knew the risk. He knew we'd mess up. But He gave us the choice anyway—because He wanted real relationship, not robotic religion.

And He still does.

Why Did God Put the Tree in the Garden?

In Genesis 2:17, God told Adam, *"You shall not eat from the tree of the knowledge of good and evil."* But the tree remained within reach. Why? Because it wasn't about the fruit—it was about love. God wanted Adam and Eve to choose Him. He gave them the dignity of choice.

As 1 John 3:4 says, *"Sin is the transgression of the law."* The word "transgress" means to go beyond a boundary. Adam was given a clear boundary. Eve wasn't yet created when the law was given, which means Adam had the responsibility to teach it—and perhaps he added to it ("Do not touch"). When the added part was broken and there were no immediate consequences, it likely made it easier to also ignore the original command. That's the danger when we treat God's boundaries lightly.

God doesn't force us to love Him. **His commands are not cold demands; they are opportunities to respond to His love.** Like Jesus said: *"If you love Me, keep My commandments."* (John 14:15)

Think of it like this: if someone says they love you but consistently does what hurts you, is that love? No. God's laws are not about control—they're a way to live in relationship with Him. He is Love and to respond to his love is to obey His commandments given to man.

The Power and Progression of Sin

Sin isn't just a decision—it's a **power**, a spiritual force that enslaves when continually indulged. James 1:14-15 gives us a clear roadmap:

"Each person is tempted when they are dragged away by their own evil desire and enticed. Then, after desire has conceived, it gives birth to sin; and sin, when it is full-grown, gives birth to death."

Sin starts small—an enticing thought, a casual compromise. But if it's fed, it grows. Just like with addiction.

Consider the story of Timmy. The first time he smoked, he coughed and hated it. But he forced himself past that feeling, violating his own will. That act **activated the power of sin.** Soon, it wasn't a choice anymore—it was a compulsion. Teddy, who began drinking in a similar way, hardened his will to keep doing it until it took over. At that point, **they were no longer free.**

When deliverance came—when God intervened—the power was broken. They could say "no" again. But temptation didn't disappear. Now it came dressed as **deception**: "Try it again. You're stronger now. You've changed." And if they yielded, they felt defiled... dirty... too far gone.

Sin deceives. Then it defiles. Then it enslaves. Then it torments. What once felt pleasurable becomes torture. And without intervention? It leads to destruction.

Your Teen Has the Power to Choose

Parents, your teen is standing at this same edge. Maybe not with cigarettes or alcohol—but with lust, lies, laziness, pride, or fear. Sin always starts with a decision. But they **still have the power to say no**.

Your role is to help them see that their choices matter—and that God's grace gives them strength to choose well.

John 8:36 reminds us: *"If the Son sets you free, you will be free indeed."*

Biblical Stories That Show the Weight of Choice

The Bible is full of people at crossroads:

- **Joseph:** Betrayed but faithful—he chose integrity, and God honoured it. (Genesis 37–50)

- **Samson:** Strong but reckless—he chose pleasure over wisdom and paid the price. (Judges 13–16)

- **Ruth:** Loyal and obedient—her faith led her into the lineage of Jesus. (Ruth 1–4)

- **Saul:** Obedient in small things—he was just looking for donkeys, but God made him king. (1 Samuel 9)

Each one had a choice. And so does your teen.

Your Job Is Not to Control—It's to Coach

You can't walk into every classroom or friendship with your teen, they might not even want you. But you can be the voice that echoes in their heart when they're alone.

Instead of saying, "Don't do that!" try asking:
- "What does God's Word say about this?"
- "How will this decision shape your future?"
- "Is this leading you closer to who God made you to be?"

Teens don't need micromanagers. They need wise guides.

Final Word: Love Must Be Chosen

Real love always involves risk. God knew Adam might sin—but He also knew that without the freedom to choose, **love would never be real**.

Likewise, your teen might mess up. They might walk into pain. But they might also rise, with resilience and purpose, because they know they were trusted... and loved.

Teach them that God's commands aren't fences to restrict them, but doors to deeper relationship. Help them see that every choice is a response to love—and an invitation to live in freedom.

Because in the end, love that is chosen freely is the kind of love that changes everything.

Chapter 2
Building a Foundation of Trust
Creating Safety for Honest Conversations

Have you ever wondered why your teenager pulls away... even when all you're trying to do is help?

You're not alone.

Building trust with teens is like constructing a bridge—one conversation, one reaction, one small choice at a time. It's a process that demands patience and understanding. But here's the hard truth: that bridge can take months or even years to build... and just one moment of anger, sarcasm, or control can put a deep crack in it.

Still, there's hope.

In God's story, broken trust is never the end. It's an invitation to rebuild.

The Trust Struggle Is Real
Teenagers live in a strange tension—craving freedom while quietly longing for security. They may not say it out loud (some days they barely grunt at all), but beneath the rolled eyes and awkward silences, they're constantly wondering:

- *Are you safe to talk to?*
- *Can I mess up and still be loved?*
- *Will you actually listen—or just lecture?*

You've likely seen it already—the slammed doors, the one-word answers, the increasing distance. Maybe you've thought, *What happened? They used to tell me everything.*

But here's what's easy to forget: behind that wall is a heart still watching, still wondering, still hoping you'll stay close even when they push away.

We've all been there—biting our tongue when they push buttons, fighting the urge to panic when they confess something raw. And it's in those very moments that trust either grows... or quietly fades.

Real-Life Story: The Listening Dad

Marcus could feel something wasn't right with his 15-year-old son, Jordan. Dinner had become painfully quiet. The bedroom door was always closed. And when he tried to ask questions, Jordan gave nothing but shrugs.

The old version of Marcus? He would've kicked that door open and demanded, *What's going on with you?* Maybe even taken away his phone or grounded him at that time "until he was able to talk."

But this time around ... he chose something different.

He invited Jordan for a drive. No expectations. No hidden agenda. Just space.

For a while, it was just the hum of the road and the occasional sigh. But slowly, Jordan opened up.

1. Struggles with Friends

Jordan finally admitted that some of his close friends were changing. They were vaping, ditching class, and mocking him for still caring about grades or church.

"They're not bad people, Dad... but I don't want to be like them anymore."

Marcus didn't shame him or start lecturing about peer pressure. Instead, he asked gently,

"What kind of man do you want to be a year from now? And who's helping you get there?" This simple question not only stuck but also highlighted the crucial role parents play in guiding their teens towards the right path.

That simple question stuck.

Together, they made a plan: Jordan would still be friendly but started sitting with different kids during lunch. He'd quietly distance himself from the group chats and started joining a weekly youth hangout at church instead.

It wasn't easy—he felt the sting of being left out. But he also discovered new friends who shared his values in a way that was practical for him to identify with. Over time, he learned that choosing integrity doesn't always feel good at first—but it leads to peace of heart.

2. Questions About Faith

As they drove past a quiet church, Jordan spoke up again.

"I don't even know if I believe this stuff anymore."

He'd been watching videos online from various sources — some were sceptical, some mocking Christianity—and they stirred up real doubt in his heart.

Marcus could've panicked. But instead, he breathed deeply and said, "You're allowed to ask questions. God's big enough to handle them—and so am I."

They started listening to faith podcasts together. They read short passages of Scripture and talked about what confused them. And Jordan started asking:

- *How do we know God is real if we can't see Him?*
- *Why does God allow bad things to happen?*
- *What if I believe in God but still have doubts sometimes?*

Marcus didn't try to have all the answers. He modeled curiosity and faith in process. They found answers in Scripture—and in silence, prayer, and walking the road together.

That didn't "fix" everything. But it gave Jordan a very powerful message: *Doubt isn't a dead end. It's part of the journey—and I'm not walking it alone.*

3. Fears He Didn't Know How to Voice

Then came the most vulnerable moment.

"I don't think I'm enough. I feel like I keep letting everyone down."

Jordan had been carrying a silent weight—from expectations at school, from youth group leadership, from his own desire not to disappoint his parents. He felt like he was juggling everything... and dropping all of it.

Many teens feel this way: the pressure to perform, to be perfect, and not to make mistakes. Especially the quiet ones. They often internalise the stress until it starts showing up as anxiety, shutdowns, or anger.

Marcus didn't try to solve it. He simply put a hand on his shoulder and said,

"You don't have to be perfect to be loved. I'm proud of who you are, not just what you do."

That night didn't change everything. But it planted something. A seed of security. A quiet assurance that when the pressure mounts, he's not alone.

Modern Story: The TikTok Secret

Emma, a mom of three, was scrolling on her daughter Lily's phone one night when she stumbled on her TikTok videos. Some were harmless dances—but others made her stomach twist. Not inappropriate... just too revealing. Too grown.

Old Emma would've grabbed the phone and shut it all down.

But instead of reacting impulsively, she paused. She waited. That weekend, over ice cream, she said gently,

"What do you love about making those videos?"

Lily's face softened. "It's just fun. It's how I express myself. And some of them... they're about encouraging people. I didn't tell you because I thought you'd just say no."

That hit Emma really hard. Not because of the videos—but because of the fear behind them.

She realized that, If her daughter was afraid of her reaction, she might stop sharing altogether.

So instead of shutting it down, they made a plan. They talked about what was appropriate. They decided on privacy settings. And Lily invited her mom to be part of her creative process.

The result? Deeper trust. Because curiosity—not control—built connection.

Jesus' Example: A Safe Space at the Well

In John 4, Jesus met a woman carrying shame, silence, and secrets. And instead of judging her, He started with a question:

"Will you give me a drink?"

He didn't shame her past. He invited her into conversation.

And that conversation changed everything.

Our teens don't need interrogations. They need invitations—simple questions that open doors to deeper honesty.

What Breaks Trust: The Controlling Parent

Sarah loved her daughter deeply—but fear drove her parenting. One night, when her daughter left her phone unlocked, Sarah read her texts.

She told herself it was for safety. But when her daughter found out, the silence was deafening. Doors locked. Secrets multiplied. Conversations dried up.

Control might feel protective—but it often communicates this: *"I don't trust you."*

And teens? They'd rather confide in friends—or the internet—than feel micromanaged by fear.

Another Story: When Over-Control Backfires

Matt's son, Ethan, stayed out late one night without checking in. Matt panicked and responded with rules, apps, and lectures.

It didn't make Ethan safer. It just made him sneakier.

Eventually, Matt realized: He wasn't leading his son—he was cornering him. So he shifted from *cop* to *coach*.

Instead of tracking his every move, he started having weekly "check-in" coffees. No interrogation. Just "How's your heart?" And slowly, Ethan started opening up.

Why Trust Beats Control—Every Time
God doesn't use fear to lead us. He invites us.

He guides with truth—but always with grace.

Our teens need the same.

- **Control says:** "You'll never grow unless I control you."
- **Trust says:** "You're growing—and I'm right here with you."

They'll mess up. But the way we respond teaches them: *Am I safe here... even in failure?*

Quick Brain Science Moment
Teen brains are still under construction—especially the parts that manage impulse control, emotional regulation, and long-term thinking.

So when they make a choice that leaves you shaking your head, remember: It's not always rebellion. Sometimes it's just *incomplete wiring*.

You're not just parenting a teenager. You're helping a human finish building their brain.

That's why your steady, calm, grace-filled presence is lot more powerful than any rule.

Practical Ways to Build Trust
- **Ask open-ended questions:**
- "What's something that made you laugh today?"
- "What's stressing you out right now?"
- **Stay calm under pressure:**
- When your teen confesses a mistake, don't panic. Say,

"Thank you for telling me. Let's figure this out together."
- **Balance freedom with accountability:**
- Give them choices—but set expectations.

"You can go, but I'd like a check-in halfway through."
- **Model honest faith:**
- Let them see your own struggles and prayers. That's what makes faith real—not just rules.

When Trust Gets Broken (Because It Will)
We all mess up—parents and teens alike. When that happens:

1. **Own your part.**

"I overreacted. That wasn't fair to you. I'm sorry."

Humility softens hearts faster than demands.

1. **Let natural consequences teach.**
2. You don't have to double down. Life often does the teaching. Your job is to stay close.

3. **Rebuild slowly.**

4. Trust is rebuilt through small, faithful moments—not overnight fixes.

Biblical Reminder: Peter's Restoration

Peter denied Jesus three times. If anyone cracked trust, it was him.

But when Jesus rose, He didn't shame Peter. He made him breakfast. He asked,

"Do you love me?"

That simple act—grace over guilt—restored a relationship and empowered Peter's future.

Your "breakfast by the sea" might be a quiet drive, a late-night milkshake, or a moment of unexpected grace.

Reflection for You, the Parent

- Where is trust strong with your teen?

- Where is it shaky—and what's one step you could take to rebuild?

- Where is God inviting you to lead like Him—faithful, kind, and full of grace?

A Simple Prayer
Lord, help me reflect Your steady, trustworthy love to my teen. Teach me to guide, not control. Make me safe for their honesty, and faithful in my response.

You're Not Alone in This
Jason, a dad of two, remembers what he calls "the silent season." His kids barely spoke to him. The connection was really cold.

But instead of giving up, he leaned into small moments. Burgers. Hikes. A quick "I'm proud of you" after a rough day.

It wasn't fast and he wasn't hoping that it will be. It wasn't perfect either but he kept at it. But over time, the silence gave way to stories.

And it can for you, too.

You don't have to parent perfectly. Just faithfully.

God is with you—in the awkward, the honest, the eye-roll-filled spaces. And every small, grace-filled moment builds the bridge of trust a little stronger.

Chapter 3
Instilling Godly Values
Building a Compass for Life

"Train up a child in the way he should go; even when he is old, he will not depart from it."
— Proverbs 22:6

Raising teens in today's world can be or feel like trying to steer a boat through a storm. Achievement. Image. Popularity. Social media. They're all over the place everywhere.

And beneath all that noise, we have our teens who are quietly wondering:

"What really matters?"
That's where *godly values do* come in, to know what matters. Not as rules to follow, but as a compass for life. A grounding force. A quiet strength that helps them stay centred when the world pulls them in every direction.

But values don't stick just because we say the right things. They take root in the raw, unscripted, everyday moments where life is messy and real. These moments, often overlooked, are the true building blocks of character development which is crucial, and as a parent, you have the power to shape them.

Real Life: Character Over Performance

Emily's 14-year-old daughter walked into the house with her shoulders slumped. She didn't pass the test she'd studied for all week. But there was something else.

"I could've cheated," she whispered to herself, "but I didn't. I just... failed honestly is it not."

Emily had a choice. She could focus on the grade or on what mattered.

She hugged her daughter and said,

"That test score doesn't define you at all. Choosing integrity when no one is watching? That's what defines you. That's what lasts."

In that moment, Emily didn't just comfort her daughter. She discipled her—planting the truth that *character matters more than image*. This realization can serve as a guiding light for parents, motivating them to focus on the correct values.

What Happens When Image Comes First

James loved watching his son play soccer. But over time, his cheers only came when his son scored a goal. Not when he passed selflessly. Not when he played hard but lost. Just when he "performed."

Slowly, his son stopped enjoying the game. He stopped sharing struggles. He started associating his worth with his achievement.

"If I don't win, I'm not enough."

What began as innocent enthusiasm had quietly sent the wrong message.

When success matters more than *who they're becoming*, we risk raising performers instead of people of character.

Why Values Need More Than Words

Teenagers are in a stage of identity formation. Neuroscience confirms what parents already know: their brains are wired for figuring out, *"Who am I?"*

And while culture screams messages of comparison, competition, and compromise, your life is quietly answering that question for them every single day.

Your voice.

Your responses.

Your example.

More than lectures, it's your *life* that teaches.

Six Godly Values That Anchor Teens (and How to Model Them)

Let's examine six godly values that shape a strong moral compass—and see how both Scripture and real teens today embody them in action.

1. Honesty
Bible Role Model: Joseph (Genesis 39)

Joseph was offered power, comfort, and secrecy when Potiphar's wife tried to seduce him. But he chose truth, even though it cost him everything. He said:

"How could I do such a wicked thing and sin against God?"

Modern Teen Story: Aiden's Confession
Aiden, 17, made a mistake during an online test. He clicked where he shouldn't have. Guilt ate at him. The next day, he told his teacher. She was stunned—but really moved by his action. His truthfulness and honesty earned him much respect and sparked a lot of onversation about integrity in the school.

How Parents Can Model It:
- Admit when *you're* wrong.

- Celebrate honesty even when it's uncomfortable to accept.

- Say, "Thank you for telling me the truth. That means more than getting it right."

2. Humility
Bible Role Model: Moses (Numbers 12:3)

Despite leading thousands, Moses was described as *more humble than anyone on earth.* He didn't chase credit. He depended on God.

Modern Teen Story: Maya's Apology
Maya, 15, snapped at her youth leader during a group activity. Later, she apologized publicly. Everyone saw her apologise.

"I was having a bad day, but that doesn't excuse how I acted. I'm sorry for snapping at you."

That moment spoke louder than any sermon.

How Parents Can Model It:
- Say, "I overreacted. That wasn't fair."
- Let your kids see you ask for forgiveness from them and others too, making it easier for then to do same when they need to..
- Remind them: strength isn't in pretending to be right, but in owning when you're wrong.

3. Respect
Bible Role Model: David (1 Samuel 24)

David had every reason to strike Saul—but he didn't. He honoured Saul's position, even when Saul didn't act honourably.

Modern Teen Story: Caleb and the Coach
Caleb disagreed with his basketball coach's call, but instead of yelling, he asked for a conversation afterwards. His calm respect opened a door, and the coach later told his parents, "He's the kind of leader teams need."

How Parents Can Model It:
- Speak kindly to service workers in front of your kids so they can have a visual aid.

- Don't belittle others—even those you disagree with.

- Expect respect—but give it in return.

4. Gratitude
Bible Role Model: Paul (Philippians 4)

In prison, Paul wrote about the importance of contentment. He thanked God, not because life was easy, but because grace was enough.

Modern Teen Story: Nia's Gratitude List
After struggling with anxiety, She was always focusing on the things that she did not have and things she could not do but she decided to change. Nia began writing three things she was thankful and grateful for every day. Slowly, peace replaced pressure. Her family noticed her joy shifting and joined her in the practice.

How Parents Can Model It:
- Say "thank you" often—to your teen, to your spouse, to God.

- Model thankfulness at meals, in prayer, and during times of crisis.

- Keep a gratitude journal together—or share weekly highlights at dinner.

5. Responsibility
Bible Role Model: Nehemiah (Nehemiah 2-6)

Nehemiah didn't wait for someone else to fix the problem. He owned it. He planned, led, and worked—brick by brick, day by day.

Modern Teen Story: Eli's Lawn Business
Eli, who is 16years old, started mowing lawns to save for college. He missed hangouts, faced setbacks, and sometimes considered quitting. But he stuck with it. His parents didn't do it *for* him—they cheered him *on*.

How Parents Can Model It:
- Let teens own their chores—and their consequences.

- Resist the urge to rescue too quickly.

- Say, "I believe you can handle this—and I'm here to help if you need it."

6. Faith
Bible Role Model: Timothy (2 Timothy 1:5)

Paul praised the sincere faith passed down from Timothy's grandmother and mother—a faith that wasn't inherited by words alone, but was evident in *how they lived*.

Modern Teen Story: Sofia's Quiet Boldness
Sofia, 17, started a Bible verse series on Instagram. It wasn't flashy, but it was real. One friend DM'd her saying,

"I've been doubting God for a while... but your posts remind me He's still there."

How Parents Can Model It:
- Let your teen see you pray—even when you're unsure.
- Discuss *your* questions and how God is guiding you.
- Invite them into your faith, not force them into rules.

Letting Values Take Root: Everyday Moments Matter
You don't need to craft perfect devotionals or give TED Talks at bedtime. Most of the time, the best discipleship happens in the in-between.

A car ride after a hard day
A quiet moment after a mistake (yours or theirs)
A comment during a movie or a headline on the news
A walk where silence leads to something sacred

It's less about having all the right words... and more about showing them what living *God's way* looks like in real time.

Reflection for You, the Parent

- Which values does your teen already reflect well?
- Where might they need extra grace and guidance?
- Do your actions align with the values you want them to learn?
- Choose *one value* this week to intentionally model—start small. Stay consistent.

A Simple Prayer

Lord, help me live the values I want to see in my teen. Let honesty, humility, and faith flow from my life first. When I fall short, please help me to lead with grace. And remind me that every seed planted in love, you will grow in time.

You're Not Alone in This

You may not see immediate fruit. Your teen might roll their eyes or tune you out. But the seeds are being planted. And in God's time, they will take root.

You don't have to raise perfect kids. Just point them toward a perfect Saviour.

And as you do? You're not only shaping their future... you're shaping their faith.

Chapter 4
Helping Your Teen Stand Tall in a World That Pulls Them Down

"Do not be conformed to this world, but be transformed by the renewal of your mind..."
— **Romans 12:2**

Let's be real—the pressure teens face today isn't just "peer pressure" the way we remember it. It's **constant**, it's **digital**, and it's **emotional**.

They're bombarded every day:

- TikTok trends that decide what's "cool"—and what's cringe.

- Group chats that throw shade at anyone who brings up faith.

- Silent but strong messages: *"Just go along. Don't make it awkward. Don't stand out."*

We can't remove the pressure. But we can prepare them to stand tall in it.

Daniel Faced It Too

Think about Daniel.

A teenager, likely 15 or 16, when his whole world was upended. Dragged to Babylon—far from home, stripped of his culture, given a new name, new food, new language, and surrounded by a godless system that said, *"Conform or be crushed."*

But Daniel had something the others didn't: **a secret life with God**.

He prayed three times a day. He sought God's voice when no one was watching. His private devotion gave him **divine insight**, **inner peace**, and **unshakeable clarity**. Daniel didn't just resist pressure—he received supernatural wisdom.

If Daniel lived today? He'd be the kind of teen who sees beyond the drama, reads the room spiritually, and could probably guess someone's phone passcode—*not by hacking, but because the Holy Spirit gives him insight the world can't explain.*

His story shows us: **Courage isn't about being loud. It's about being lit up inside with truth.**

When your teen knows how to *stay close to God*, they'll begin to *see clearly*—not just what's popular, but what's *right*.

The Modern Daniel: Real Courage in Real Life
Sophia's Quiet Stand

Sophia, 15, started getting excluded from hangouts because she didn't go along with the party scene. Some of her old friends started teasing her, calling her "church girl" and "goody two-shoes."

It stung. She cried bitterly when she was alone. She wondered if staying true to her values was worth the loneliness.

But her parents didn't panic. They listened to her very carefully. They prayed with her. They said, *"God doesn't call you to fit in. He calls you to shine."*

And little by little, Sophia found real friends who respected her boundaries and shared her beliefs. Her courage? It grew. And so did her confidence.

That's what happens when *home becomes a safe place to wrestle and recover*. It helps teens stay tall when the world tries to shrink them.

When Silence Speaks Louder Than Truth

Jamal's parents took him to church. They loved God. But they never talked about real issues—peer pressure, sex, identity, faith in public.

So when kids mocked Jamal for saying he didn't believe in hookup culture, he didn't know what to do. He stayed quiet. Then he started slipping—first in small ways, then big ones.

The world filled the silence his parents left behind.

Honest conversations at home don't protect kids from pressure.

They *prepare* them to face it.

The Truth About Belonging
Teens do crave connection and God has designed it that way. They're asking:

"Where do I fit? Who am I becoming?"

That's not weakness—it's human. But when *belonging* matters more than *truth*, that's when compromise sneaks in.

Your job isn't to bubble-wrap them. It's to **anchor them in love and identity** so that when pressure comes, they know:

"I don't have to shrink to be accepted. I don't have to blend in to be loved."

How to Build Courage in Your Teen—One Small Step at a Time
You don't need a degree in youth ministry. You just need to **be intentional** in the little things.

1. Share Your Stories
Talk about your own teenage battles. The mistakes. The moments you caved. And the moments you didn't.

When they hear, "I've been there," it makes space for them to be honest, too.

2. Role-Play Tricky Situations
Ask, *"What would you do if a friend sent you something inappropriate?"*

Or *"What if someone laughed at your faith?"*

Help them script out godly responses *before* the moment comes. It gives them courage in real time.

3. Spot the Subtle Stuff Together
Not all pressure is drugs and parties. Sometimes it's:
- Liking certain posts to stay liked.
- Laughing at a joke that hurts someone.
- Staying silent when someone disrespects their values.

Train their eyes to quickly and always recognize pressure in its sneaky forms, so they can know what to do.

4. Give Them Language to Say No
Practice saying:
- "That's not for me."
- "Nah, I've got other plans."
- "I respect your choice, but that's not who I am."

Those simple sentences become shields.

And When They Mess Up? Grace Still Stands

Even Daniel had friends who got thrown into fire for doing the right thing. Your teen might face heat too. And yes—they'll sometimes *give in* to pressure.

But your response in those moments will teach them more than any rule ever could.

Don't explode.

Don't shame.

Just be present. And point them back to grace.

"One moment doesn't undo your identity. God's mercy is fresh today."

Reflection for You, the Parent

- Where is your teen feeling the squeeze to blend in?

- Have you talked about your own challenges with peer pressure?

- What's one way—this week—you can encourage their courage?

You don't need to fix everything overnight. Just keep showing up. Keep speaking truth. Keep anchoring them in God's love.

A Simple Prayer

Lord, help my teen stand when it's easier to shrink.

Let Your truth be louder than culture's lies.
Give them a heart that seeks You, ears that hear You,
and courage to follow You—even when it's hard.
And when they fall, remind them: You're still right there, arms open.

One Last Reminder: Seeds Are Being Planted

You might feel like they roll their eyes at every "talk."

Like your encouragement goes in one ear and out the other.

Like nothing's working.

But don't give up.

Even when you can't see it—**God is watering every seed.**

Every word of truth. Every prayer you've whispered. Every late-night conversation where you just listened.

He's growing something strong in them.

They might not stand tall every day. But they'll remember where the ground is solid—and they'll come back to it.

You're not raising a perfect teen.

You're raising a *rooted one*.

Chapter 5
Why Wisdom Matters
Teaching Your Teen to Choose Wisely

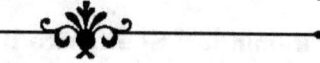

"Wisdom is the principal thing; therefore get wisdom..." — **Proverbs 4:7**

Start Here: Why Talk About Wisdom?

Dads, let's be real: there will be moments in your teen's life when you're not there to help.

You won't always be in the room when the temptation shows up, when the decision has to be made, or when the pressure hits hard.

But God has already made a way for your teen to thrive—even in those moments. That way is called **wisdom**.

And if you're going to raise a teenager to choose wisely, they have to understand what wisdom is, why they need it, and how to seek it.

1. What Is Wisdom?
Wisdom is the **ability to solve problems God's way**.

It's not just knowing information—that's knowledge. Wisdom is knowing **what to do**. It's practical, directional because it gives direction, and grounded in truth.

Let me break it down like this:
- **Knowledge** says: "Sugar is bad for your health."
- **Wisdom** says: "So don't eat that second doughnut."

See the difference?
- **Knowledge informs. Wisdom guides.**
- **Knowledge tells you what's happening. Wisdom tells you what to do next.**

2. Why Is Wisdom So Necessary?

Because—this might surprise you—you and your teenager were **made insufficient**.

That's not a design flaw. It's part of God's design.

He is all-sufficient. We are not. And that's intentional—so we will run to Him.

If we had all the answers, we wouldn't seek God for direction. But life reminds us again and again: **we need wisdom beyond ourselves**.

3. Sam's Story: When Insufficiency Hits

Let me tell you about a young man named Sam.

He was sharp. Educated. Had money. A great family. Things were going well.

Then came a personal crisis—a serious relationship issue that rocked his identity. He called friends, read books, switched churches—nothing helped.

It didn't destroy him. But it exposed him.

For the first time, he realized:

"I don't have what it takes on my own."

That's when something shifted. He stopped trying to fix it himself. He turned to God, by praying and asked for wisdom on how to fix it practically. That moment of humility was the turning point for him.

4. Problems Are Meant to Lead You to God

God doesn't allow problems to crush us. He allows them to bring us closer to him as we will need His help and wisdom as input to solving the problem.

Your teen will face those moments too—the kind that knock the wind out of them:

- A breakup they never saw coming and did not prepare for

- A friend or colleague who turns their back without warning

- Academic pressure that builds until it feels like they can't breathe

- A decision that spirals into real-life consequences

And in those moments—when they feel confused, hurt, or even ashamed—you won't always be there to step in to give your input or fix it.

But you can prepare them now.

Train them to recognize this truth:

"This problem doesn't mean I've failed.

It means I need wisdom—and God is inviting me to ask for it."

Because problems aren't the end of the story.

They're the place where wisdom begins to grow.

5. Wisdom Is God's Antidote to Your Limits

Problems aren't always the result of sin or poor choices. Sometimes, they're simply proof that we're human beings.

And God has given us an answer:

"If any of you lacks wisdom, let him ask of God... and it will be given to him." — James 1:5

God isn't stingy with wisdom. But He gives it **to the humble**—those willing to say, "Lord, I don't know what to do. Show me."

6. Train Your Teen to Ask the Right Question

Many teens get stuck asking questions like, *"Why is this happening to me?"*

Instead, help them start asking:
- *"What is God teaching me through this?"*
- *"What wisdom do I need to move forward from this experience?"*

That shift—from **victim thinking** to **wisdom-seeking is how to** transform how they approach every challenge.

7. Final Thought for Fathers: Wisdom Is Transferable
You won't always be there to make the choice for them. But you can give them something better:
- **Knowledge** about life
- **Example** through your own humility
- **Training** in how to seek God's voice

When your teen sees you stop and ask God for wisdom, it gives them permission to do the same. Share your own experiences of seeking wisdom from God with your teen, and encourage them to do the same.

Summary: Teach Your Teen This Truth
"Wisdom is the ability to solve problems—and it comes from God."

Help them understand:
- Problems aren't proof of failure
- Their limits are invitations to seek God
- Wisdom isn't automatic—it's asked for
- God gives it to those who humbly ask

This is how you raise a teenager to **choose wisely**.

Reflection Questions for Your Teen
- When was the last time you faced a problem you couldn't solve on your own?

- What did it reveal about your limits?

- Have you ever stopped to ask God for wisdom? What happened?

- What's one area right now where you could use wisdom?

Prayer to Close With Your Family
"Father, thank You for showing us that we are not enough on our own—and that we don't have to be. You are all-sufficient, and You promise to give us wisdom when we do ask. Teach us to come to You first when we face problems so we can expreince your wisdom. Let our hearts be humble, our ears open, and our feet ready to follow where wisdom leads. In Jesus' name, amen."

Chapter 6
Anchoring Your Teen's Heart in Godly Wisdom

"The integrity of the upright guides them, but the crookedness of the treacherous destroys them."
— ***Proverbs 11:3***

The Challenge: Raising a Teen in a Shifting World

Let's be honest—raising a teenager today can feel like trying to build a house during an earthquake. One minute your teen is laughing at dinner, dreaming about college or starting a new project with excitement... and the next, the ground beneath them (and you) seems to shift.

- A friendship suddenly ends over a misunderstood text.

- Social media quietly convinces them they're not enough.

- They start to question their identity, their faith, even their future.

And you, the parent, are left asking: *What just happened?*

It's overwhelming. You want to fix it, to step in and make everything steady again—but you can't always be there. And even when you are, they don't always want to hear it from you.

So what do you do?

The Hope: God's Wisdom Is Steady Ground

Here's the good news: God's wisdom doesn't shake, shift, or fade with trends. It's timeless. It's personal. And it's powerful enough to guide your teen through every high and low they may be faced with in their journey.

Proverbs isn't just a book of ancient advice—it's a practical manual for navigating the chaos of modern life with grace and truth. It anchors both you and your teen when emotions run high and answers feel few.

Why Teens Need Godly Anchors

Ephesians 4:14 paints the picture clearly:

"Then we will no longer be immature like children. We won't be tossed and blown about by every wind of new teaching..."

That's what we're seeing, isn't it? Teens tossed by trends, confusion, peer drama, and pressure. Not because they're weak—but because they're still figuring it all out.

They need more than rules. They need **wisdom**.

Wisdom teaches them to:
- Stand firm when peer pressure heats up

- Make decisions based on the truth, not just feelings
- Walk in humility instead of pride
- Speak with kindness, even when others don't do it.

And it all begins with the fear of the Lord—not terror, but awe and deep reverence. The kind that makes them pause and say, "God, what do *You* think about this?"

Encourage them to go deeper with this through solid resources like *"Fear of the Lord"* by Bukky, helping them understand that true wisdom flows from knowing who God is—and respecting Him enough to follow His lead.

Teaching Teens to Listen to the Inner Witness

One of the most powerful gifts God has placed in your teen is the inner witness of the Holy Spirit.

It's not loud.
It's not dramatic.
And it's definitely not always logical.
But it's always protective.

As a parent, you've likely worried about the choices your teen might make when you're not around. But here's a peace-giving truth: **God has already put within every believing teen a spiritual warning system**—a quiet "no" that whispers before danger comes close.

The challenge isn't whether God is speaking. It's helping our teens recognize that voice and trust the voice.

Sin: Not Just Adam's Problem

Teens need to understand this crucial truth: **they're not judged for Adam's sin—but for their own choices.**

Romans 6:23 says, *"The wages of sin is death,"* not because of some inherited curse, but because of personal rebellion. Teens aren't condemned for someone else's fall—but they are responsible for their own decisions.

And that's not just weighty—it's freeing.

Because if they are responsible, they are also empowered.

Empowered to choose well.

Empowered to say no.

Empowered to listen to the Holy Spirit and walk in life.

Why Teens Fall Into Deception

1 John 2:26 warns us:

"I am writing these things to you about those who are trying to lead you astray."

Deception doesn't just "happen." It comes when someone ignores the voice of the Spirit.

Here's the pattern:

1. A teen feels a discomfort in their spirit—an uneasiness.

2. Then, their mind starts rationalizing it:
    - "It's not that bad."
    - "Everyone's doing it."
    - "I'm probably overreacting."

3. They override the prompting—and make a decision that leads to regret.

That's why we must teach them this simple but life-saving principle:

"If I don't feel right about it, I don't do it."

No explanation needed. No proof. Just peace—or the lack of it.

That sense of inner discomfort *is* the Holy Spirit waving a flag.

Story: Debby—Saved by a Whisper

Debby had just come to Christ a few months earlier. After school one day, a friend invited her to the park. It seemed harmless. But Debby had started to pay attention to the gentle nudges of the Holy Spirit.

As she checked her heart, she felt a quiet unease. Then a single word dropped into her spirit: **"Thief."**

Confused but cautious, she declined the invite.

Later, she learned the girl had been caught trying to shoplift—and had planned to involve Debby.

She could have walked into legal trouble and shame. But she didn't. Because she didn't joke with the whisper.

She walked in the light—and the light protected her.

Story: Lydia—Rescued by the Light
Lydia's story was different. She was a believer, too, but the danger she faced wasn't as obvious.

A friend invited her to join a plan to make easy money. Lydia didn't feel a strong warning, so she said yes.

What she didn't realize was that it involved fraud. By the time she understood what was happening, she was already entangled.

But even in her mistake, **God didn't abandon her**.

That night, during Bible reading, truth lit up the situation like a spotlight. She saw it clearly. She broke. She repented.

And God restored her.

Helping Your Teen Stay Sensitive to the Spirit
Here's the heart of it for parents: **you can't control every moment, but you can help your teen stay sensitive to God.**

Here's how:

1. **Teach that obedience starts with peace.**
2. When peace leaves, something's off. That's the signal.
3. **Train them not to argue with the Spirit.**
4. It's the mental debate that leads to compromise.
5. **Affirm that they *can* hear God.**
6. The Spirit isn't reserved for adults. If they belong to Jesus, they hear Him.
7. **Keep them in God's Word.**
8. It's the light that exposes hidden traps—just like it did for Lydia.
9. **Remind them that grace still pursues.**
10. Even when they mess up, God doesn't give up. He restores. He redeems.

Wisdom in Everyday Struggles

The book of Proverbs meets your teen in the everyday:

- **Gossip in the group chat?**

"The tongue of the wise brings healing" (Proverbs 12:18).

- **Peer pressure at a party?**

"The prudent see danger and take refuge" (Proverbs 22:3).

- **Social media comparison?**
- *"A heart at peace gives life..." (Proverbs 14:30).*

Your teen's not going to get it all right. But with the Word as their compass and the Spirit as their inner witness, they'll have what they need to make wise, godly choices.

Practical: The 31-Day Proverbs Challenge

Want to anchor your family in wisdom? Try this:

1. **Pick a daily time**—5 minutes is enough.
2. **Read one chapter of Proverbs** (there are 31!)
3. **Talk briefly**—what stood out? What does it mean?
4. **Pray together**—ask God for wisdom.

Real Story: The Thompsons' "Proverbs Moment"

The Thompson family do have two teens, two tired parents—started reading Proverbs over dinner.

At first, it was awkward. Eye rolls. Grunts. But they stuck with it.

Weeks in, their daughter remembered a verse before snapping at a friend. Their son owned up to a mistake instead of lying. Slowly, wisdom took root.

"It's not perfect," their mom says, "but those 5 minutes keep our family anchored."

Wisdom Grows in Ordinary Moments

Your teen won't always remember what you taught them in a lecture—but they'll remember how you lived.

When you:
- Apologize instead of justify
- Choose patience over snapping
- Ask God for wisdom out loud

...you're showing them what it means to live Proverbs in real life.

Final Encouragement

Parenting teenagers is a very sacred, messy, and stretching labour. But here's what's so true:
- God's wisdom can steady them.
- His Spirit can guide them.
- His grace can cover what you miss out on.

Teach your teen to listen to that still, small voice. Help them treasure wisdom. And when they say, "I don't feel right about this... so I won't do it," know this:

You haven't just raised a teen who is a rule-follower.

You've raised someone led by the Spirit.

You've given them discernment.

You've given them safety.

And that?

That will carry them farther than you ever could.

Chapter 7
Raising Deliverers
Preparing Teens to Choose Wisely in a Dark World

"I know him..." — **God's Confidence in a Father**

"For I have chosen him, so that he will direct his children and his household after him to keep the way of the Lord..." — **Genesis 18:19 (NIV)**

God's Confidence in a Father

God made a remarkable statement about Abraham—not because of his wealth, achievements, or charisma, but because He knew Abraham would raise his children well.

That speaks volumes about how seriously God takes **fatherhood** and **spiritual legacy**.

Abraham wasn't just a man of faith—he was a father who would **pass down faith**. His obedience, trust, and covenant walk with God would shape Isaac. Isaac would shape Jacob. Jacob would father the twelve tribes.

God was laying a foundation through one obedient father— a man who would **train his children to choose wisely** in a corrupt culture.

And God is still looking for fathers and mothers like that today.

God Knew What Was Coming

"Know for certain that for four hundred years your descendants will be strangers in a country not their own... but afterward they will come out with great possessions." — Genesis 15:13–14

God wasn't surprised by Egypt or Pharaoh. He saw it all in advance:
- 400 years of slavery
- Pharaoh's cruelty
- A nation in bondage
- A deliverer already rising in His plan

And in the same way today—God sees:
- The rise of digital addictions
- Gender confusion
- Pornography
- A generation crying out

But He's not panicked. He's **raising deliverers**—and He's doing it through parents like you.

But Why Did God Allow Such Evil?

It's a question many still ask:
- *Why did God allow Pharaoh to rule with cruelty?*
- *Why does He allow today's cultural chaos?*
- *Why is this generation so attacked?*

Here's the sobering truth:

God may allow darkness to rise—but He always raises deliverers in parallel.

Sometimes, He lets the world get darker to display His power through **young people who've been discipled in truth**.

Moses: A Deliverer in Training

When Pharaoh commanded, *"Throw every Hebrew boy into the Nile,"* he didn't know he was funding God's plan.

Because the very law meant to destroy Moses became the first step in preparing him.

Just like in:
- Judas' betrayal which led Jesus to the cross
- Pilate's injustice brought salvation
- Pharaoh's palace became Moses' classroom

God was orchestrating every moment.

The Divine Setup: Every Step Aligned

Let's break it down:

- **A Mother's Obedience**

- Jochebed who was Moses' mother placed him in a basket. What if she hesitated? What if she delayed?

- **A Sister's Watchfulness**
- Miriam was close by—ready to speak at the right time.
- **A Princess's Timing**
- Pharaoh's daughter "just happened" to be there. Her heart "just happened" to be moved.

Nothing was accidental. God orchestrated every detail.

And Moses—ironically—was **raised by the very system he would one day confront**:
- Pharaoh paid for his food
- Financed his education
- Trained him in leadership, strategy, and power

God placed Moses inside the system to study it—so he could later **lead people out of it**.

Why Education Wasn't Enough

Moses had:
- **Access**
- **Influence**
- **Power**
- **Privilege**

But when the time came, he **walked away from it all**:

"By faith Moses, when he had grown up, refused to be known as the son of Pharaoh's daughter... He

chose to be mistreated along with the people of God." — **Hebrews 11:24–25**

Why?

Because in those first 5 to 7 years of his life, **his mother planted a foundation of truth**.

But she didn't just nurture him — **she drilled his identity into him**.

While Egypt called him a prince, **she reminded him, "You are not an Egyptian... you are a Hebrew. You are God's child. You were born for something greater."**

She didn't have years of influence, but she made the most of the time she had. And what she spoke into Moses' heart in those early years stuck with him for life.

He wasn't confused about who he was.

When the palace tried to rename him...

When Pharaoh's daughter tried to adopt him into power...

When culture tried to shape him...

He already knew who he was.

And **this is what we, as parents, are called to do**:

We must speak clearly and confidently into our children's identity — **before the world gets a chance to lie to them**.

We get the sacred privilege of shaping what our children believe about themselves:

- "You are not your failures."
- "You are not your feelings."
- "You are not what the world calls you."
- **"You are chosen. You are loved. You are God's."**

Let's not underestimate the power of what we declare over our children.

The palace may offer them comfort, but it cannot offer them clarity.

That must come from home.

Even if you only have a few years — make them count.

Even if you feel outnumbered by culture — plant the truth anyway.

Even if they don't always seem to listen — **keep speaking life**.

Because one day, they'll face a crossroads like Moses did.

And if the foundation is there, **they'll know which road to choose.**

That foundation taught him to **choose suffering with God's people over comfort with Pharaoh**.

Parents—take note:

You don't need perfect children.

But you **must plant truth before the world plants lies**.

Mentoring vs. Discipleship
Egypt mentored Moses.

But **his mother discipled him**.

And later, when he fled to Midian, **Jethro didn't just mentor him—he discipled him too**.

There's a big difference:
- **Mentoring** equips with skills.
- **Discipleship** forms the heart.

Story: Two Coaches, Two Outcomes

Marcus was a talented high school athlete—smart, disciplined, and fast. Everyone believed he'd get a scholarship. His track coach, Coach Willis, saw the potential early on and invested heavily in him.

Coach Willis mentored Marcus very well:
- Taught him how to train his body
- Showed him how to push through pain
- Helped him polish his resume and ace college interviews

Marcus became one of the top runners in the state. Scholarships rolled in. On paper, he was thriving.

But behind the scenes, Marcus was crumbling.

He was dealing with anger, insecurity, and private struggles he didn't know how to talk about.

Coach Willis cared deeply about Marcus's success—but **never asked him about his soul.**

Then came Coach Reggie.

He wasn't officially part of the team, just a volunteer from Marcus's church who helped with weekend training. He noticed something was off and began checking in.

Not about running.

Not about school.

About life.

He asked real questions:
- "How's your heart?"
- "What's weighing you down?"
- "Have you talked to God about this?"

Over time, Marcus opened up more to him about what was happening. Reggie prayed with him. Challenged him to forgive his absent father. Taught him how to spend time in the Word. Shared how he overcame similar struggles as a teen.

And slowly, **Marcus changed**.

Not just his mindset—but his heart experienced a change.

Two Men. Two Approaches.
- **Coach Willis mentored Marcus.**
- He helped him succeed on the track.
- **Coach Reggie discipled Marcus.**
- He helped him walk with God.

The Lesson for Parents
Mentoring equips with skills.

Discipleship **forms the heart**.

Both matter. But only one will still guide your teen when the crowd is gone, the scholarship fades, or the pain hits.

Discipleship gives them something no mentor ever can—a personal, growing, resilient relationship with Jesus Christ.

Through Jethro, Moses didn't just learn how to lead—**he learned how to listen**.

He discovered:
- **Humility**
- **Spiritual leadership**
- **How to hear God's voice**
- **How to lead people, not just systems**

Jethro wasn't a warrior. He wasn't training Moses to fight like Pharaoh's army.

He was a priest—training Moses to lead like a servant.

And here's the truth:

Moses needed both.

He needed the excellence of Egypt, **but also the spiritual depth of Midian.**

He needed Pharaoh's exposure **and** Jethro's discipline.

Because gifting without grounding is dangerous.

Now, Think About Today's Teens

Today's world offers our kids **plenty of mentorship**:

- School teaches them how to succeed.
- Coaches teach them how to perform.
- Social media "influencers" mentor them constantly—how to dress, think, speak, and even feel.

But few are truly **discipling** them.

- Who's helping them develop humility?
- Who's teaching them to hear God's voice?
- Who's showing them how to lead people with compassion, not just confidence?

That's **our job as parents**.

We're not just raising performers, influencers, or high-achievers.

We're raising **deliverers**—and they need **discipleship**, not just direction.

Mentors may prepare them for success in the world, but discipleship prepares them to stand firm in it.

Our teens don't just need help **getting ahead**—they need help **getting rooted**.

That kind of formation doesn't come from the palace.

It comes from **home, church, and consistent spiritual guidance.**

So Here's the Call:
Don't just mentor your teen to be excellent.

Disciple them to be godly.
- Help them build spiritual habits.
- Walk with them through failure with grace.
- Challenge their character, not just their GPA.
- Speak into their purpose, not just their performance.

Because when the pressures of Pharaoh's palace rise—and they will—it won't be their talent that helps them choose wisely.

It will be their training in truth.

Body, Soul, and Spirit: Raising the Whole Teen

In my book *101 Tips for Child Development*, I talk about developing children in:

- **Body and intellect** (education)
- **Soul** (emotions and habits)
- **Spirit** (their connection to God)

Here's the reality:

A well-educated teen might become a successful person.

But only a spiritually formed teen can become a deliverer in God's hands.

Who Is God Calling You to Raise?

Maybe it's your son.

Maybe it's a teen at your church.

Maybe it's a foster child or your grandson.

Whoever it is—don't just raise them to behave.

Raise them to **hear God's voice**.

Raise them to **stand in dark times**.

Raise them to **choose wisely** when the culture pressures them to compromise.

Lessons for Parents and Guardians

- **Plant spiritual foundations early** — like Moses' mother. You may only have a few years.
- **Trust God's orchestration** — He's aligning moments you can't yet see.

- **Teach your child to seek God's voice** — talent and education won't be enough.

- **Disciple them, don't just mentor them** — immerse them in truth, not just experiences.

Final Thought: Pharaoh Is Still Throwing Boys in the Nile

Only now, the Nile looks like:
- **Social media** that feeds insecurity and comparison
- **Pornography** that rewires desire and numbs the soul
- **Gender confusion** that distorts identity
- **Gaming addiction** that isolates and consumes
- **Apathy and unbelief** that silence spiritual hunger

And let's be real—**there is nothing that deflates and discourages a teen like sexual sin**.

Why? Because sexual sin doesn't just affect behavior—it touches identity.

It **deflates** their spiritual momentum.

They start to pull back from prayer, worship, and community. They feel like they've lost something inside—like the spiritual air has been sucked out of their confidence.

And it **discourages** them at the heart level.

Many teens begin to believe the lie that they're too far gone, too dirty, or too broken to be used by God. They carry quiet shame, and instead of running to God, they hide.

Sexual compromise doesn't just damage their choices—it **erodes their identity.**

That's why it's so important that we, as parents, create safe spaces for truth and grace. We must teach our teens that **failure isn't final**, but it **must be faced**. God doesn't shame them—He restores them. But we have to guide them back to truth before culture cements the lie.

Shame wraps around them. Confidence shrivels. Purpose fades.

Sexual compromise doesn't just hurt their future—it **undermines their identity**.

But here's the hope:

God doesn't throw teens away because of failure.

He raises deliverers from broken places.

Even Moses was born under a death sentence. Even he ran in fear after messing up.

But God still used him mightily—**because someone discipled him before Egypt could define him.**

And He's still doing it today.

God Is Still Raising Deliverers

Yes, Pharaoh is still at work.

But so is God.

And He's still looking for parents—**like Abraham**—He can trust with the next generation.

> *"I know him... he will direct his children to keep the way of the Lord."* — **Genesis 18:19**

Challenge for You, Parent:

Will God say the same about you?

Will you be the voice of truth **before** culture becomes the louder voice?

Will you raise a teen who knows who they are—**even when the world tries to rename them?**

Will you disciple them deeply, not just mentor them casually?

Because here's the truth:

The world doesn't need more high performers.

It needs more spiritually grounded teens who will live on mission for God.

Teens who know who they are, and **Whose** they are.

Let that be the legacy you build.

Not just a successful child—but a faithful one.

Not just a good kid—but a deliverer.

Chapter 8
"Proverbs in Real Life:
Stories to Inspire and Guide Teens

Wisdom isn't just ancient words — it's lived out daily in real moments. Friendships tested, peer pressure mounting, identity shaken, integrity on the line **— Proverbs comes alive in all of it.**

These short, real-life stories help teens connect timeless truth to the choices they face every day. Each story includes a verse from Proverbs, a relatable scenario (such as dealing with academic pressure, navigating family conflicts, or managing mental health challenges), reflection questions, a simple prayer, and a tip for parents.

Mason's Integrity Moment

Proverbs 12:22 — "The Lord detests lying lips, but He delights in people who are trustworthy."

Mason, who is a 16-year-old boy, found himself in a tough spot when he accidentally broke his neighbor's window while playing baseball. His first instinct *was to run away so that no one sees him,* but his conscience wouldn't allow it. He went to tell his parents what had happened. With much courage and strength, he went and he knocked on the neighbor's door, admitted his mistake to them, and they were not even aware and with the help of his parents, he made it right. The respect he earned was a testament to his courage and strength.

Reflection:
- Have you ever been tempted to hide a mistake that you made?
- How did your choice affect your peace?

Prayer:
God, help me choose honesty, even when it's hard.

Parent Tip:
Share a moment when telling the truth was tough for you — and how it built trust. Then, discuss with your teen how they can navigate similar situations with honesty and integrity.

2. Sophie's Social Media Stand

Proverbs 29:25 — "Fear of man will prove to be a snare, but whoever trusts in the Lord is kept safe."

Sophie, a 15 years old girl, felt the pressure — friends daring her to post wild videos to get followers. *"Everyone's doing it, you'll go viral!"* But she remembered: her worth comes from God, not likes. She passed, lost a few followers... but gained confidence and real friends who respected her.

Reflection:
- What pressures do you feel online?
- How do you remind yourself of your real worth?

Prayer:
Lord, help me care more about Your opinion than the crowd's.

Parent Tip:
Discussing the pressures of social media and setting very clear boundaries together can help to provide a sense of security and protection. These boundaries can help protect your worth and identity, there by ensuring that your online presence reflects your true self.

3. Mia's Gossip Exit

Proverbs 16:28 — "A perverse person stirs up conflict, and a gossip separates close friends."

Mia is a 14 years old girl, watched her friend group tearing others down with gossip. It felt toxic. *"I don't want to be part of this."* She walked away and sought friends who build people up. It was lonely at first, but real, kind friendships followed.

Reflection:
- How do you react when friends gossip?
- What kind of friendships do you want?

Prayer:
Lord, help me speak words that heal, not hurt.

Parent Tip:
Model positive speech. Show your teen how avoiding gossip builds stronger, kinder friendships.

4. Dylan's Cheating Temptation

Proverbs 10:9 — "Whoever walks in integrity walks securely, but whoever takes crooked paths will be found out."

During finals, Dylan's high school friends sent test answers in a group chat. His phone buzzed. *"It'd be easy... no one would know."* But Dylan knew better. He chose the harder path, the path of honesty. He studied really hard and he took the test honestly, it was very tough for him, but he had peace in his heart after he had done his best. Some of his friends got caught cheating—Dylan's integrity protected him.

Reflection:
- Have you been tempted to cut corners?
- How does doing the right thing affect your self-respect?

Prayer:
Dear God, please grant me grace and I ask for your daily guidance and strength to stay very true, even when shortcuts seem tempting and enticing to me.

Parent Tip:
Celebrate effort and honesty over just grades. Remember, integrity lasts longer than test scores, and it's the key to a bright future.

5. Liam's Peer Pressure Party

Proverbs 1:10 — *"My son, if sinful men entice you, do not give in to them."*

Liam, 16, got invited to a party with drugs and alcohol. His friends teased, *"Don't be boring!"* But he had a secret code with his dad. One text—his dad called with an excuse to pick him up. Liam left, teased a little, but with his choices and future very intact.

Reflection:
- How do you handle pressure to do wrong?
- Who's your safe person to call?

Prayer:
God, give me courage to say no when I need to.

Parent Tip:
Create "safe words" for your teen to use when they need help exiting risky situations.

6. Emma's Envy Battle

Proverbs 14:30 — *"A heart at peace gives life to the body, but envy rots the bones."*

Emma, is a 15 years old girl who, was scrolling through flawless social media posts—perfect bodies, dream vacations, constant success. *"Why don't I have that?"* Envy crept in. She decided to limit her scrolling and focus on gratitude. Slowly, peace replaced comparison.

Reflection:
- When have you ever felt jealous before?
- What can you remember that helped you appreciate your own life?

Prayer:
Lord, help me trade envy for gratitude and peace.

Parent Tip:
Talk about comparison traps. Celebrate your teen's unique strengths and worth.

7. Caleb's Humble Win

Proverbs 27:2 — *"Let someone else praise you, and not your own mouth; an outsider, and not your own lips."*

Caleb, is a 17 year old boy who, dominated the basketball season—everyone noticed him and he did not want to be noticed. Social media buzzed. His friends bragged for him, but Caleb stayed humble. He let his hard work and character do the talking for him, which was able to earn him more respect than any boast could.

Reflection:
- How do you respond to praise?
- Why does humility often earn more respect?

Prayer:
God, help me stay grounded in success and let my actions speak.

Parent Tip:
Model humility—praise effort and character over flashy accomplishments.

8. Natalie's Truth-Telling Test

Proverbs 19:1 — *"Better is the poor whose walk is blameless than a fool whose lips are perverse."*

Natalie, 14, accidentally broke her friend's necklace. That made her to be very fearful. *"I could lie..."* But she told the truth. Her friend was really upset but appreciated her honesty—and trust between them grew stronger.

Reflection:
- Have you ever been scared to tell the truth?
- How did honesty affect your relationships?

Prayer:
God, help me be truthful, even when it's uncomfortable.

Parent Tip:
Create every space you can for honesty by showing grace when your teen messes up.

9. Ethan's Wise Dating Boundaries

Proverbs 4:23 — *"Above all else, guard your heart, for everything you do flows from it."*

Ethan, 19 in his second year of college, started dating—his friends teased him for setting boundaries. *"That's for little kids!"* But Ethan and his girlfriend made very clear choices to protect their hearts, which was seen by their colleagues. Their relationship thrived on respect—without any form of regrets.

Reflection:
- What boundaries matter to you in relationships?
- How does guarding your heart help long-term?

Prayer:
Lord, help me protect my heart and honor You in relationships.

Parent Tip:
Talk openly about dating, boundaries, and respect—listen more than lecture.

10. Sophia's Reaction to Criticism
Proverbs 15:1 — *"A gentle answer turns away wrath, but a harsh word stirs up anger."*

Sophia, 15, got unfairly blamed after a group project. Her first thought? *"I'll snap back."* But she took a breath, then decided to respond gently, and the argument de-escalated. Her calmess did earn respect and resolved the issue.

Reflection:
- How do you react to unfair criticism?
- What could change if you decide to respond calmly?

Prayer:
God, help me stay very calm and use gentle words.

Parent Tip:
Model calm responses in conflict—show your teen how words can build peace.

11. Noah's Financial Wisdom

Proverbs 21:5 — *"The plans of the diligent lead to profit as surely as haste leads to poverty."*

Noah is an 18 year old boy, he got his first paycheck—and almost blew it all. But he paused, budgeted, saved, and even gave some away. His friends joked, but when surprise expenses hit, Noah's planning paid off.

Reflection:
- How do you manage money?
- What benefits come from saving and planning?

Prayer:
Lord, teach me to handle money with wisdom and generosity.

Parent Tip:
Involve your teen in real budgeting talks—share both your wins and mistakes.

12. Olivia's Forgiveness Moment

Proverbs 17:9 — *"Whoever would foster love covers over an offense, but whoever repeats the matter separates close friends."*

Olivia, is a 15 year old girl, who felt crushed when her best friend betrayed her trust. She did not watch as bitterness grew, but she desired for peace. Olivia chose forgiveness as her option. It wasn't easy, but grace slowly rebuilt their friendship and her own peace.

Reflection:
- How do you handle being hurt by someone close?
- What can forgiveness free you from?

Prayer:
God, give me a forgiving heart—help me let go and heal where there is unforgiveness.

Parent Tip:
Share your experiences with forgiveness, so that it can help and let your teen see grace in action.

Proverbs isn't just for ancient times. It's for the choices teens make today—for integrity, courage, peace, and a life that reflects God's wisdom.

Real-Life Story #13: James's Pride Check
Proverbs 16:18 — *"Pride goes before destruction, a haughty spirit before a fall."*

Positive Choice:
James is a 17 years old quiet boy, who was known for being the science genius at school. His shelves overflowed with medals, and his head started to swell too. He found himself looking down on others, thinking he had all the answers. But

when he bombed a big test, reality hit hard. That failure—and Proverbs—humbled him. James owned his attitude, apologised to his classmates, and refocused on learning. In the end, his humility made him not just respected but also a better leader.

Negative Example:
When pride takes over, it's easy to lose friends and face embarrassing downfalls.

Reflection Questions:
- Have you ever allowed success to make you feel better than others?
- How can humility help protect your character?

Prayer:
God, please help me to stay very humble, even when I succeed. Keep my heart open to correction and growth.

Parent Tip:
Share a time pride tripped you up—and how humility restored you. Show your teen that true confidence comes with kindness.

Real-Life Story #14: Hannah's Friendship Filter

Proverbs 13:20 *— "Walk with the wise and become wise, for a companion of fools suffers harm."*

Positive Choice:
Hannah, is a 15 year old girl , faced a tempting offer when the 'cool crowd' invited her to join them. But she quickly realized that their choices were not in line with her values. Reading the book of Proverbs guided her to make a difficult decision, but one that led to real friendships that strengthened and uplifted her, giving her a sense of empowerment and confidence.

Negative Example:
Choosing friends without careful consideration can lead you into situations you'll regret.

Reflection Questions:
- What qualities do you really want in your friendships?
- How do wise friends help you grow?

Prayer:
Lord, help me choose friends who build me up and honour You.

Parent Tip:
Discuss very openly the impact of peer pressure and friendships. Help your teen spot the difference between uplifting friends and those who bring trouble.

Real-Life Story #15: Marcus's Tech Boundaries

Proverbs 25:28 — *"Like a city whose walls are broken through is a person who lacks self-control."*

Positive Choice:
Marcus, 16, loved gaming—but it started stealing his sleep, grades, and even his mood. He realised his life felt like a city without walls: wide open to chaos. Inspired by Proverbs, Marcus set gaming limits, took breaks, and rebuilt his focus. Life beyond the screen came back into view—friends, school and peace.

Negative Example:
Without setting boundaries, habits can spiral, leading to burnout and isolation.

Reflection Questions:
- Where do you think you will need better boundaries in your life?
- How does self-control help you thrive?

Prayer:
God, give me the strength to control my habits and honour You with my daily choices.

Parent Tip:
Help your teen set realistic screen-time limits. Encourage more balance with activities that build real-world connection

Real-Life Story #17: Zara's Overcoming Anxiety

Proverbs 3:5-6 — "Trust in the Lord with all your heart and lean not on your own understanding; in all your ways submit to Him, and He will make your paths straight."

Positive Choice:
Zara, 16, dreaded class presentations. Her heart would race, her hands did tremble, and panic would set in. She felt trapped by her anxiety. But instead of giving up, she prayed—and remembered Proverbs. Trusting God didn't instantly erase her fear, but it gave her enough courage to take a step. She showed up. With each moment of faith, her fear lost a little power, and her confidence grew. After she had finished with the presentation, the relief she felt was so huge, giving her a reminder that faith doesn't always take fear away, but it gives us strength to move through it.

Negative Example
Trying to handle fear alone can leave you feeling stuck, drained, and defeated.

Reflection Questions:
- What fears are holding you back right now?
- How might things shift if you trusted God with them?

Prayer:
God, help me face my fears with You by my side. Help me to see you in it. Even when I'm afraid, give me courage to keep moving forward.

Parent Tip:
Make it normal to talk about anxiety. Share a moment from your own life when fear was real—but faith helped you through. It helps teens see they're not alone.

Real-Life Story #18: Logan's School Pressure Moment

Proverbs 23:4 — *"Do not wear yourself out to get rich; do not trust your own cleverness."*

Positive Choice:
At 17, Logan was juggling top grades, scholarship deadlines, and a packed schedule—surviving on caffeine and barely any sleep. It felt like he was doing everything *right*, until his body and mind hit a wall. Total burnout. That's was when his study of the book of Proverbs reminded him: nonstop hustle doesn't equal success. Logan began to value rest and balance. He reshaped his schedule, got more sleep, and started trusting God with his future instead of trying to control everything himself.

Negative Example:
Pushing yourself beyond your limits might seem like the way to great success, but it can leads to burnout, exhaustion, and a whole lot of stress.

Reflection Questions:
- Have you ever felt at any time that you are like you're drowning in pressure or expectations?
- What would change if you trusted God more with your future?

Prayer:
Lord please, help me find a healthy balance between working hard soo hard which i have to do and resting well. I want to give my best, but I also want to trust You with the outcome.

Parent Tip:
Model healthy rhythms. Talk with your teen about the dangers of burnout, and help them create space in their schedule for rest, fun, and faith.

Real-Life Story #19: Bella's Friendship Break-Up

Proverbs 18:24 — "One who has unreliable friends soon comes to ruin, but there is a friend who sticks closer than a brother."

Positive Choice:
Bella, 15, started noticing that her friend group was all about gossip, risky choices, and tearing others down. She knew it didn't feel right—but walking away was tough. It meant being alone for a while. Still, Proverbs reminded her: not all friendships are meant to last. Eventually, she found someone who respected her values and who help to build her up. That loneliness faded, replaced by a deeper friendship built on trust and kindness.

Negative Example :
Staying in toxic friendships might feel easier than walking away—but over time, they can drag you down and leave you feeling empty.

Reflection Questions:
- Are there any type of friendships in your life right now that are pushing you away from your goals?
- What makes someone a real or loyal friend to you and not just in words, but in how they show up for you?

Prayer:
God, give me the courage to let go of friendships that hurt me and the wisdom to find those that bring me closer to You.

Parent Tip:
Share your own experiences with friendships that ended or evolved. Help your teen learn to recognise the difference between surface-level connections and friends who genuinely care.

Real-Life Story #20: Eli's Respect for Parents Moment

Proverbs 1:8-9 — *"Listen, my son, to your father's instruction and do not forsake your mother's teaching. They are a garland to grace your head and a chain to adorn your neck."*

Positive Choice:
Eli who is 14 years old, often rolled his eyes at his parents' "old-school" rules. They felt outdated and annoying—until the moment he was pressured by friends to skip school and try drugs. Suddenly, his parents' warnings came rushing back. He walked away from the situation, and in that

moment, he realized their rules weren't to punish him but they were there to protect him. That choice helped him avoid regret, and opened his eyes to the wisdom in their guidance.

Negative Example:
It's easy to ignore advice we don't want to hear—but turning away from wisdom often leads to mistakes we can't undo.

Reflection Questions:
- How do you usually react when your parents set limits you don't like?
- Can you remember a time their advice actually protected you?

Prayer:
God please, help me respect the wisdom my parents do offer—even when it's hard to hear. Help me see their love through their guidance.

Parent Tip:
Don't just give rules—explain the *why* behind them. Let your teen know your boundaries come from love, experience, and a desire to protect them from mistakes you've learned the hard way.

Real-Life Story #21: Jasmine's Dating Discernment

Proverbs 4:7 — *"The beginning of wisdom is this: Get wisdom. Though it cost all you have, get understanding."*

Jasmine's Story:
Jasmine, 16, was flattered when a charming guy started paying her attention at school. He was funny and confident—but how he treated others? Not so great. Her friends did encourage her, by saying, "You deserve someone who notices you!" But deep down, Jasmine sensed something wasn't right. Remembering Proverbs, she asked God for wisdom at that point. It wasn't easy for her, but she chose to walk away, holding out for someone with real respect and character.

The Other Side:
Chasing attention without paying attention to red flags often ends in hurt and regret.

Reflection:
- What really matters to you in someone you date?
- How does God's wisdom help you see beyond charm?

Prayer:
Lord, give me your wisdom to wait for relationships that honor You—and me.

Parent Tip:
Talk openly about dating and self-worth. Remind your teen, their value isn't based on who notices them—but on who they already are in God's eyes.

Real-Life Story #22: Gabriel's Confidence Struggle
> *Proverbs 31:30* — *"Charm is deceptive, and beauty is fleeting; but a woman who fears the Lord is to be praised." (True for everyone—guys and girls.)*

Gabriel's Story:
Gabriel, 15, couldn't stop comparing himself to others. Social media made it worse for him—he didn't feel "cool enough," "strong enough," or "good-looking enough." But when he read the book of Proverbs, it hit him and knew that real worth isn't about likes or looks. Gabriel started focusing on kindness, courage, and his God-given talents. Slowly, his confidence grew—not from the world, but from within.

The Other Side:
Measuring your worth by appearance or popularity drains your joy and peace.

Reflection:
- Where do you look for your sense of worth?
- What helps you remember you're already valuable to God?

Prayer:
God, help me see myself through Your eyes—loved, capable, enough.

Parent Tip:
Limit social media when possible. Celebrate your teen's character, talents, and strengths beyond appearance.

Real-Life Story #23: Leah's Betrayal Moment

Proverbs 20:22 — "Do not say, 'I'll pay you back for this wrong!' Wait for the Lord, and He will avenge you."

Leah's Story:
When Leah's best friend shared private messages with others, she felt crushed—and furious. Part of her wanted revenge, to expose the friend's secrets too. But Proverbs reminded her—let God handle it. Leah stayed quiet, forgave in her heart, and gave the situation to over to God. Over time, the truth came out, and Leah's peace stayed intact.

The Other Side:
Revenge feels good for a moment—but it usually makes things worse.

Reflection:
- How do you usually handle betrayal?
- What would trusting God's justice look like for you?

Prayer:
God, help me forgive those who hurt me and trust You to make things right.

Parent Tip:
Teach your teen that forgiveness brings much freedom, even when it's hard. Share your own stories of letting go.

Real-Life Story #24: Evan's Digital Detox
Proverbs 25:16 — *"If you find honey, eat just enough—too much of it, and you will vomit."*

Evan's Story:
Evan, 17, found himself stuck in the loop—scrolling TikTok, gaming for hours, bingeing YouTube. His mood tanked, his grades slipped, and life just felt...empty. But he remembered that Proverbs had showed him: even good things in excess can make you sick. Evan set screen time limits, immediately and swapped some online time for real-life connections. His joy and energy came back.

The Other Side:
Too much screen time steals your focus, mood, and relationships.

Reflection:
- How much time do you spend on screens?
- What boundaries could help you feel more alive?

Prayer:
God please, help me to set healthy boundaries and enjoy life beyond the screen.

Parent Tip:
Work together to set tech limits that is practical. Encourage offline hobbies, friendships, and real-world fun.

Real-Life Story #25: Kara's Humble Moment
Proverbs 11:2 — *"When pride comes, then comes disgrace, but with humility comes wisdom."*

Kara's Story:
When Kara, 15, won a national art contest, the praise rolled in—and pride whispered in her ear, "You're better than them." But Proverbs reminded her—stay humble. Kara thanked those who supported her, encouraged younger artists, and kept her focus on glorifying God, not on herself. Her success felt even sweeter.

The Other Side:
Allowing pride take over, isolates you and dims your light.

Reflection:
- How do you handle compliments or even achievements?
- How can humility make success even more meaningful?

Prayer:
Lord, help me stay humble and grateful, giving You the credit for every good thing.

Parent Tip:
Celebrate wins, point out the team behind the success, model humility, gratitude and courage

Real-Life Story #26: Nathan's Time Management Wake-Up

Proverbs 21:5 — *"The plans of the diligent lead to profit as surely as haste leads to poverty."*

Nathan's Story:
Nathan, who is 16 years old, was the king of procrastination. Big project due? He'd always wait until the night before with panic, and then scramble. His grades—and confidence—suffered. But reading the book of Proverbs taught him a better way: steady, small steps. Nathan started making simple to-do lists and setting reminders. It wasn't perfect, but stress faded, and his grades (and peace) improved.

The Other Side:
Procrastination steals your peace and sets you up for failure.

Reflection:
- What's one task you've been avoiding?
- How could small daily steps make life easier?

Prayer:
God, help me be to be disciplined and use my time wisely to honor You.

Parent Tip:
Break big projects into bite-sized tasks with your teen. Celebrate more of effort, not just outcomes.

Real-Life Story #27: Emily's Integrity Test
Proverbs 10:9 — "Whoever walks in integrity walks securely, but whoever takes crooked paths will be found out."

Emily's Honest's Story:
During a math test at school, whispers filled the room with answers being shared amongst the students. Emily, 14, knew she could cheat and probably not get caught. But a witness, something within reminded her that integrity matters more than given in. She stayed honest, even when it felt very lonely. Later, her teacher praised her for standing firm—and others quietly respected her too.

The Other Side:
Cheating might feel like a shortcut, but it damages your character and trust.

Reflection:
- Have you been pressured to compromise your values?
- What has helped you to stay honest even when it was tough?

Prayer:
Lord, give me the strength to choose integrity, even when no one's watching.

Parent Tip:
Share your own experiences with peer pressure and integrity. Your honesty gives your teen courage.

Real-Life Story #28: Jake's Rejection Reframed

Proverbs 3:26 — "For the Lord will be your confidence and will keep your foot from being snared."

Jake's Story:
Getting cut from the basketball team crushed Jake so badly at 17 years old. He felt very humiliated and doubted his abilities. But Proverbs reminded him— true confidence doesn't come from achievements, but from God. Instead of giving up at that time Jake trained harder, joined another team, and built resilience. His faith and confidence grew stronger through the setback.

The Other Side:
Letting rejection define you can steal your confidence and joy.

Reflection:
- How do you handle rejection or failure?
- Where does your real confidence come from?

Prayer:
God, remind me that my worth isn't based on wins or losses—but on You.

Parent Tip:
Normalize failure as part of growth. Remind your teen God's love and purpose don't change with circumstances.

Real-Life Story #29: Sophie's Modesty Choice
Proverbs 31:25 — *"She is clothed with strength and dignity; she can laugh at the days to come."*

Sophie's Story:
Sophie who is a 15 years old girl, got invited to a party, and the pressure was real—"Show some skin, fit in, get attention." But Proverbs reminded her: true beauty comes with strength and dignity. Sophie chose an outfit that reflected her confidence and self-respect. Some teased her, but her quiet strength turned the right kind of heads.

The Other Side:
Giving in to peer pressure can hurt your self-worth and how others see you.

Reflection:
- How do you show strength and dignity in how you present yourself?
- What choices reflect respect for yourself and God?

Prayer:
Lord, help me carry myself with confidence, strength, and dignity that honors You.

Parent Tip:
Talk openly about peer pressure that is so common and self-image. Encourage your teen's worth beyond looks or trends.

Real-Life Story #30: Isaac's Quiet Influence

Proverbs 27:17 — *"As iron sharpens iron, so one person sharpens another."*

Isaac's Story:
Isaac who was a 16 years old boy, saw his friend drifting away by skipping church, making sketchy choices. He could've ignored it, but having read Proverbs reminded him that real friends sharpen each other. Isaac shared his own struggles, invited his friend to church, and kept showing up. Over time, his friend opened up—and started making better choices.

The Other Side:
Staying silent when friends struggle can let bad habits grow.

Reflection:
- How can you be a positive influence on your friends?
- When is it hard to speak truth with love?

Prayer:
God, help me lovingly encourage my friends and be an example of Your grace.

Parent Tip:
Teach your teen that influence happens through love, not lectures. Celebrate small moments of impact.

Real-Life Story #31: Max's Hidden Apps Exposed

Proverbs 28:13 — "Whoever conceals their sins does not prosper, but the one who confesses and renounces them finds mercy."

Max's Story:
Max who is a 17 years old boy who thought he was being smart—sneaking apps his parents banned. But a tech-savvy teacher noticed, and Max's secret unraveled fast. Fear and shame overwhelmed him. Remembering what he had learnt from reading the book of Proverbs, Max confessed to his parents. The conversation was complicated, but healing started. He realized: hiding mistakes traps you—but honesty sets you free.

The Other Side:
Secrets weigh you down. Truth, even with consequences, brings peace.

Reflection:
- Have you ever hidden something and felt like you were stuck?
- Why is honesty worth it, even when it's uncomfortable?

Prayer:
God please, give me much courage to be very honest and walk in truth, no matter what I am confronted with.

Parent Tip:
Model vulnerability. Share times you messed up and how confession brought peace.

Real-Life Story #32: Mia's Party Pressure
Proverbs 1:10 — "My son, if sinful men entice you, do not give in to them."

Mia's Story:
The music was very loud, drinks were everywhere, and people whispered, "Don't be lame—just take only one sip." Mia who was 16 years old, felt the pressure. Her heart raced, but Proverbs echoed in her mind: *don't give in*. She quietly texted her parents their secret "bailout code" and left. Some friends teased her, but later, they respected her courage—and her clean record.

The Other Side:
Giving in to pressure feels very easy in the moment but often leads to regret and much trouble. Standing firm, on the other hand, empowers you and reinforces your real values.

Reflection:
- Have you ever felt pushed to do something against your values?

- How can you prepare your "exit plan" when things feel unsafe?

Prayer:
Lord please, give me the strength to stand firm and walk away when I need to.

Parent Tip:
Make a family "bailout plan" with code words for tricky situations. Share your own stories of peer pressure and smart exits.

Real-Life Story #33: Olivia's Social Media Reset

Proverbs 25:28 — "Like a city whose walls are broken through is a person who lacks self-control."

Olivia's Story:
Endless scrolling, comparing, FOMO—Olivia, 15, was drained. She knew she needed boundaries but felt stuck. Proverbs reminded her that self-control protects your peace. Olivia then set daily screen limits, swapped scrolling for journaling and walks, and her anxiety was lifted. Honest clear conversations did replace endless comparison.

The Other Side:
Allowing social media to control your time and emotions can often lead to stress and insecurity.

Reflection:
- How does the time you spend on your screen affect your mood and even your confidence?

- What are some healthy habits that could use to replace endless scrolling?

Prayer:
Lord please, help me develop self-control and focus on what truly matters to you.

Parent Tip:
Work with your teen to create healthy tech boundaries that are helpful. Encourage screen-free activities that spark real joy and connection.

Real-Life Story #34: Grace Stands Against Bullying
Proverbs 31:8-9 — "Speak up for those who cannot speak for themselves."

Grace's Story:
Scrolling through her feed, Grace who is 15 years old froze. A classmate was getting slammed with cruel comments. Part of her wanted to look away, but Proverbs nudged her: *Speak up.* Grace reported the posts, after she messaged support, and even suggested a kindness campaign at school. It wasn't easy, but standing up made a great difference—and others followed her lead.

The Other Side:
Staying silent when others are hurt lets the problem grow.

Reflection:
- Have you seen someone bullied? How did you react?
- What steps can you take to stand up for others safely and effectively?

Prayer:
Lord, give me the courage to be a voice for those who are unheard.

Parent Tip:
Praise your teen's empathy when it seen. Discuss openly safe and effective ways to address bullying.

Real-Life Story #35: Noah's Generosity in Action

Proverbs 11:25 — "A generous person will prosper; whoever refreshes others will be refreshed."

Noah's Story:
With his first paycheck, 16-year-old Noah dreamed of buying new pair of shoes and playing video games. But something tugged at his heart. He then went ahead and donated part of money to a local shelter. His friends teased him when they heard, but Noah's quiet generosity sparked conversations—and inspired others. Giving didn't drain him; it filled him with joy and a sense of purpose.

The Other Side:
Holding everything for yourself leaves you empty; sharing creates connection.

Reflection:
- How do you feel after helping someone?
- What simple acts of generosity could you try today?

Prayer:
God, help me live with open hands—ready to give and prepared to love.

Parent Tip:
Involve your teen in giving—whether time, talents, or money. Show them generosity in action.

Real-Life Story #36: Ava's Stress Reset
Proverbs 3:5-6 — "Trust in the Lord with all your heart and lean not on your understanding."

Ava's Story:
School deadlines. Exams. Family expectations. Ava a 17 years old girl, felt crushed by the pressure. But having read the book of Proverbs reminded her that *you don't have to carry this alone.* She paused, prayed, asked for help, and started building small moments of rest into her week. Her peace returned—so did her energy.

The Other Side:
Ignoring stress or trying to handle everything alone leads to a total burnout.

Reflection:
- What stresses you out most?
- How can leaning on God change how you face pressure?

Prayer:
Lord, help me slow down, trust You, and rest when life feels overwhelming.

Parent Tip:
Model healthy stress management—discuss prayer, routines, and seeking help.

Chapter 9
Taming Technology
Without Losing Your Sanity (or Your Teen)

"I will set no worthless thing before my eyes..."
— ***Psalm 101:3***

Instructions for Parents:
- **Read one chapter of Proverbs daily with your teen for 31 days or remind them to do so.**

- After reading, deliberately **engage in a meaningful dialogue with your teen about how the wisdom** in Proverbs applies to their world, especially in the context of technology and in their daily choices they will have to make. This dialogue is crucial for them to understand and apply the wisdom they've read to their circumstances. **Claim the promise:** Teach your teen to obey the wisdom in Proverbs, knowing it brings trustworthy guidance and lots of protection in a tech-saturated world.

Live it out: As a parent, you play a crucial role in modelling balanced tech use. Your example speaks louder than rules and can have a significant influence on your teen's behaviour. **Celebrate wins:** When your teen makes wise choices online or resists temptation, take the time to affirm and celebrate their actions. This will not only boosts their confidence but also anchors their heart in the right direction.

The Digital Age Dilemma: Keeping Sanity While Staying Connected

Parenting Let's a teen in today's digital storm feels like trying to sip water from a firehose. Notifications never stop. TikTok trends morph overnight. Group chats buzz nonstop. You want your teen to enjoy their online world, grow in faith, and connect with friends—but also protect them from the junk that sneaks in.

Banning tech outright? Unrealistic.

Guiding wise use? Absolutely doable. This approach will not only empowers you as a parent but will also instils a sense of control and confidence in managing your teen's tech use. You have the power to shape their digital habits and protect them from the potential harms of technology.

Why Technology Tempts Like the Garden's Forbidden Fruit

Remember Eve in the garden? That fruit didn't look scary or ugly—it was **pleasing to the eye** and promised wisdom (Genesis 3:6). Technology is similar: instant connection, endless entertainment, knowledge at a swipe. Parts of it are good. But when misused, it isolates, drains confidence, and pulls hearts away from God.

Real Life Balance: Isaiah's Story

Isaiah, 16, loves gaming. His parents didn't go all "no screens" or "full shutdown." Instead, they set clear boundaries that will help:

Homework first

No screens after bedtime

Tech-free meals

But they didn't stop there—they showed Isaiah how tech could **build**

faith:

- Bible apps for daily devotion
- Worship playlists during downtime
- Podcasts that encourage and inspire

This rhythm gave Isaiah freedom **without chaos and a** balance **without being burnt out**.

When Boundaries Are Missing: Lily's Story

Lily's parents thought, "She's home, so she's safe." But she was endlessly scrolling behind closed doors which led her to comparison, anxiety, and creeping insecurity. Without boundaries or check-ins, she silently drifted into self-doubt.

Technology isn't the enemy as it has come to stay, but without limits, it can quietly steal joy and peace.

Biblical Anchors in a Distracted World

David, "a man after God's own heart" (1 Samuel 13:14), was well acquainted with distraction. Surrounded by enemies and chaos, he chose to seek God's face and find refuge (Psalm 17:8). Just as David, your teen can learn to **fix their eyes on God** amidst the noise, whether digital or otherwise.

Trusting God's Step-by-Step Path: Saul's Story

God's plan unfolds one step at a time. Saul didn't start as a king—he was obeying a simple task (looking for lost donkeys). But obedience led him to Samuel, who anointed him king (1 Samuel 9–10).

If Saul hadn't obeyed that small task, he'd have missed his destiny. Your teen's obedience in small tech choices and daily faithfulness is building their path to purpose, because "it is by grace you have been saved" and God has "prepared good works for us to walk in" (Ephesians 2:8-10).

Questions to Ask Yourself & Your Teen

Before laying down rules, get curious:
- What is my teen looking for online? Escape? Approval? Fun?
- Is Technology helping or hurting their faith?
- Am I modelling healthy tech habits?

Yes, they might roll their eyes—but they want your wisdom more than you realise.

Boundaries That Protect—Not Punish

Healthy boundaries say, "I love you enough to care about what shapes your heart." Try these:

- No devices in bedrooms overnight (protect sleep and heart)
- Screen-free zones: meals, car rides, family time
- Regular check-ins: "What's new or weird on your feed these days?"

Boundaries aren't about control—they're about care.

Invite Your Teen Into the Process

Teens resist control but want respect.

- Watch a documentary about the impact of social media together.

- Discuss Philippians 4:8: what is pure, lovely, and worthy of praise?

- Let them help set boundaries—they'll take ownership of them more.

Your Example Matters Most

Your teen watches you:

- Do you scroll mindlessly or put the phone down to connect?

- Do you seek life-giving content, or do you get lost in digital noise?

- Do you demonstrate that technology can help foster faith, not just distract?

Real Story: Sarah's Turning Point

Sarah, who was a 15years old girl, found herself very stuck in the endless scroll of social media, always comparing and feeling worse about herself. Instead of lecturing, her mom got honest. She shared her own battle with phone addiction and how prayer had helped her through it. Together, they made a deal: they'd set aside time each day—no phones, just space to read scripture or talk things out.

Sarah's change wasn't an overnight thing, but her self-worth slowly moved from likes and follows to something steady, rooted in God's love.

Reflection for Parents

- Is tech building or draining your teen's faith and confidence?

- How are your tech habits shaping the family environment?

- What's one small, realistic step you can take this week toward healthier tech use?

Biblical Reminder: Moses' Mom's Trust

Parenting a teen in a tech-heavy world can feel very overwhelming. But remember Moses' mother, who placed him in a basket, trusting in God's protection (Exodus 2).

You will have to set boundaries and guide, but ultimately, **trust God's hand over their journey**.

Final Encouragement: God's Got This (and You)

You don't have to be perfect. Just show up, love well, and lead with grace. Technology is a tool. With God's wisdom and your guidance, your teen can use it for good, rather than being used by it.

Chapter 10
Overcoming Challenges Together
Walking Through Storms as a Family

*"Bear one another's burdens, and so fulfil the law of Christ." — **Galatians 6:2***

Learning to Trust God's Care — From Birds to Our Hearts

Every day, birds leave their nests trusting their Creator to provide for them. They don't worry about where their next meal will come from or where they'll find shelter. Instead, they fly freely, resting in quiet assurance. While God is not their "heavenly Father" as He is to us, He watches over them with care and kindness every single day.

One day, a young bird appeared in Caleb's garden—injured and helpless. Caleb, a thoughtful teenager, felt a gentle prompting in his heart to help this fragile creature. Even though the nearest hospital for birds was in England, Caleb was determined to get the bird the care it needed. When he first told his mother, she hesitated, unsure if it was worth the effort. But the next day, Caleb took the bird to the hospital himself.

This true story holds a beautiful lesson: If God can use a young boy like Caleb to care for a fragile bird—something small and seemingly insignificant—then indeed He will care for us, His children, who are infinitely more precious. It reminds us that we can relax and trust God's care, especially when anxiety arises about bills, problems, or an uncertain future.

The Hidden Storms Your Teen Faces

Teens often wear a confident mask. But inside, many wrestle with anxiety about school, identity, and the future; doubts about faith and self-worth; temptations from peers and social media; loneliness despite countless online "friends"; and a deep fear of rejection or not measuring up.

As a parent, you don't have to have all the answers. Your teen doesn't need perfection—they need your steady, compassionate presence through these storms.

How to Replace Anxiety with Faith: A Mother-Daughter Conversation

Biblical & Modern Stories: Facing Storms with Faith and Victory

- **Anxiety:** Elijah fled in fear and depression but found God's peace in a "still small voice" (1 Kings 19). Like Elijah, your teen can find quiet rest in God through prayer and much reflection.

- **Doubt:** Thomas doubted, but Jesus met him with patience and invitation (John 20:24-29). When your teen questions faith, respond with grace and honest conversation.

- **Temptation:** Joseph fled temptation, trusting God's plan despite risk (Genesis 39). Help your teen identify and run from temptation, seeking accountability and practical steps.

- **Loneliness:** David poured out his heart to God instead of isolating himself (Psalms 25, 42). Encourage your teen to seek authentic relationships and to bring their feelings to God.

- **Fear of Rejection:** Jesus experienced rejection but found security in God's love (John 1:11). Remind your teen that their worth is rooted in God's unwavering love for them, not in the approval of their peers.

You Are More Than a Parent—You're Their Spiritual Ally

Your teen is not just a schedule to manage or set of rules to enforce. They need someone who walks alongside them continuosly through the storms, offering grace and presence daily. When anxiety or doubt threaten, your calm and consistent support can be a lifeline.

Compassionate Responses Build Bridges

When your teen opens up—or struggles—how you respond matters deeply. Avoid harsh judgment, lecturing on vulnerability, or minimizing their pain. Instead:

- Stay calm and listen deeply.
- Affirm your unchanging love: "Nothing you say can change how much I love you."
- Ask, "How can I support you right now—spiritually, emotionally, practically?"

Jesus met people with truth and grace—you can do the same.

Teach Them Where to Run When Life Gets Hard

You can't fix every problem, but you can guide them to refuge:

- Pray *with* them, not just for them.
- Point to Scripture's honest prayers, such as those in Psalms.
- Share your own stories of God's faithfulness.
- Encourage spiritual habits, such as journaling, worship, and quiet time.

These become anchors amid life's storms.

When to Seek Extra Help
Sometimes faith and family aren't enough—and that's okay. Seek professional help if your teen's mental health worsens, if they express hopelessness or self-harm, or if they're stuck in destructive patterns.

Therapists and counsellors are tools God uses to heal. Asking for help is a sign of strength, not shame. Emphasising the vital need of seeking professional help when needed can make parents feel responsible and proactive in their role as caregivers.

Facing Storms as a Team
Storms don't have to divide you—they can unite you.
- Be honest about what's happening.
- Pray together and make plans.
- Celebrate small victories.
- Remind your teen: "I'm here for you. We'll walk this road side by side."

And remember—God is parenting you, too.

Reflection Questions for Parents
1. What storms is my teen facing right now?

2. How can I respond with more grace and presence?

3. What practical or spiritual step can we take together this week?

Real-Life Wisdom: Stories from Families
Sarah and James worried their son Michael was drifting away. Instead of lecturing, they showed up daily, praying for him, listening, sitting down quietly. Over time, Michael began opening up about fears and faith struggles that he had. Their steady presence became his anchor.

In contrast, Mark tried to control everything, and his daughter rebelled, shutting him out. The lesson? Control drives teens away. Patient, loving guidance creates space for growth.

Your Role: Guide, Not General
You don't have to have it all well figured out or control every moment. You can just share what you know with love and humility. Walk alongside your teen as they figure out their own faith journey. Trust that God has a plan, and He'll guide them in His time.

Leaving a Legacy That Lasts
Teens might forget the rules of which they will, but they'll never forget the love, grace, and faith you showed them when they were with you. One mom shared how her son, who'd been very rebellious, came back years later to thank her for never giving up on him. That's the legacy of faithful parenting—laying down a foundation that holds strong, no matter what life throws their way.

Final Encouragement for You: When It Feels Like You're Just Carrying Water — Keep Going, God Is Still Working

If you're still reading this, it probably means you care deeply—maybe even more than you know how to say it.

You're the parent standing in the hallway after another argument.

The mom crying in the car because she doesn't know what else to do.

The dad quietly wondering if he's messing it all up.

You love your teen.

But this season? It's really stretching you.

Maybe you're praying faithfully, but you're not seeing the change that you disire.

Maybe you're showing up day after day, and it feels like nothing's getting through.

Maybe your heart is quietly breaking while you keep smiling and doing laundry.

Can I remind you of something very sacred?

The Wedding at Cana — and the Water That Changed

There's a moment in Scripture that feels especially close to home for parents.

At a wedding in Cana, they ran out of wine—a big deal in that culture.

Panic was setting in. People didn't know what to do.

So they went to Mary. And Mary did what wise parents do.

She didn't panic—she pointed them to Jesus.

"Go to Him," she said.

And when they did, Jesus told them to do something very ordinary:

Fill the jars with water.

Just water. No signs, no fireworks, no instant miracle.

Just… obedience.

Can you imagine how long that must have felt?

Bucket after bucket.

Trip after trip.

And for a while, it was just water. Ordinary, heavy, unnoticed water.

But then—**somewhere along the way—it changed.**

Not because of them.

But because of **Him**.

Parenting Teens Feels Like That Sometimes

Sometimes it feels like all you're doing is carrying water:

- Saying the same prayer for the 100th time
- Choosing to stay calm after another emotional outburst
- Setting a boundary they hate—but you know they need
- Offering a hug that gets shrugged off
- Showing up to a game, or a rehearsal, or just being home when they walk in the door

It's not flashy.

It's not always noticed.

And it definitely doesn't always feel like it's working.

But **it matters**.

Because what you're doing may just look like water now…

But **God is still turning it into wine**.

God Doesn't Ask You to Do the Miracle

He just asks you to be faithful with the bucket.

You don't have to be a perfect parent.

You don't need the right words every time.

You don't have to fix your teen's heart. That's His job.

Your job?

Keep showing up. Keep praying. Keep trusting.

Even when it feels small.

Even when it feels like nothing's changing.

Because **He is doing what you cannot see**.

And If You're Wondering If It's Too Late...

Maybe your teen is far off right now. Maybe the relationship feels distant, or broken.

Can I just say: **God is not finished.**

You don't know which prayer will be the one that breaks through.

It might be the one you whisper when you're fed up.

The one you cry through on the kitchen floor.

The one you barely have words for.

But He hears.

He sees.

And **He's still working**.

You're Not Just Raising a Teenager
You're raising someone who will one day influence others.

Who will have to stand on their own.

Who will need wisdom more than popularity.

Faith more than comfort.

Conviction more than applause.

You're planting seeds—some of which you may not see bloom until years later.

So Here's the Final Word:
Keep showing up.

Keep praying.

Trust God's hand.

You're not just raising teenagers—**you're raising future men and women of God**, secure in a world that keeps shifting.

The greatest gift you can give them?

> *"The fear of the Lord is the beginning of wisdom."*
> **— Proverbs 9:10**

You carry the buckets.
Jesus does the miracle.
And one day, you'll look back and say:
"The water really did turn to wine."

Father's Teachings

Father's Teaching From David's Dad #1: Helping His Son Overcome Hidden Storms with Spiritual Wisdom

1. Anxiety Over School, Identity, and the Future

David's dad saw how anxiety clouded his son's thoughts, especially around exams and big life decisions. One night, instead of giving advice, he simply prayed with David, asking the Holy Spirit to bring peace and clarity. He did explain very slowly on how reading the Bible wasn't just about memorizing facts about the bible but training his spirit to recognize God's voice in the chaos. Together, they highlighted a verse in Jeremiah 29:11, planting seeds of hope and identity rooted in God, not just performance. David learned that day that the quiet peace that follows after prayer is God's gentle voice, a comforting reassurance that he's not alone in his fears but that God is with him at everypoint in time.

2. Doubt About Faith and Self-Worth

When David wrestled with doubts—questioning if God really cared or if he was enough for him—his father invited him to talk openly. They looked at Psalm 139 together, his father emphasized that David was "fearfully and wonderfully made." His dad shared on how doubt is a natural part of faith's journey and that God's voice often comes as a gentle whisper, not a booming shout. He encouraged David to journal scriptures that resonated with him, helping him "hear" God's voice more clearly over time, strengthening his spiritual senses.

3. Temptation From Peers, Social Media, or Other Pressures

Understanding temptation as a "voice" that can sound convincing but lead away from God, David's dad role-played real-life situations with him. They practiced saying "no" firmly but kindly and talked about the Holy Spirit as a "SIM card" in their spiritual phone—without Him, you miss the connection to God's wisdom. David began to recognize those subtle nudges—the quiet prompting to step back from a risky text or party invitation—as the Holy Spirit, a guiding presence, protecting him.

4. Loneliness, Even With Hundreds of Online "Friends"

David's dad noticed that his son's loneliness despite his online presence. He invited him to unplug for a weekend camping trip, emphasizing that God designed us for real connection. They talked about how the Holy Spirit fills the emptiness that no number of followers can. David experienced that inner peace and companionship from God's Spirit, learning that spiritual senses awaken when he chooses time with God over scrolling.

5. Fear of Rejection and Not Measuring Up
When fear of not being good enough crept in, David's father reminded him of Romans 8:38-39—nothing separates us from God's love. They practiced memorizing it together, encouraging David to whisper it when anxious thoughts hit. His dad modeled walking by faith—choosing to trust God's unseen reality over the natural feelings of inadequacy. David saw firsthand how faith activates spiritual senses, enabling him to "know" and believe God's love even when emotions scream otherwise.

Mother's Teaching from Emma's Mum #2: Guiding Her Daughter Through Hidden Storms with Heart and Spirit

1. Anxiety Over School, Identity, and the Future
Emma's mom gently listened to her worries and suggested they make a "worry box" where Emma could write down fears that she has and pray them over. She explained that consistent Bible reading is like training the spirit to recognize God's voice. They picked Proverbs for wisdom and practiced meditating on the some of the verses, helping Emma to anchor her identity in God's love rather than the shifting opinions of peers or social media.

2. Doubt About Faith and Self-Worth
Emma's mom shared her own faith doubts candidly with her, showing vulnerability and humanity. They read stories of biblical figures who wrestled with God but stayed faithful. Her mom taught Emma that spiritual vitality isn't

about knowing all the answers but about being inspired by the Holy Spirit's gentle whisper—often a quiet peace or a timely scripture that arises in the heart when needed.

3. Temptation From Peers, Social Media, or Other Pressures

Rather than issuing very strict rules, Emma's mom invited her to discuss how social media can both uplift and pressure. They created boundaries together and learned to recognize emotional triggers that often precede temptation. Emma was encouraged to pause when overwhelmed, pray quietly, and remember that the Holy Spirit's voice is gentle and peaceful—unlike the loud, demanding pressure of peers or screens.

4. Loneliness, Even With Hundreds of Online "Friends"

Emma's mother noticed her daughter's loneliness and invited her to plan intimate family dinners or invite a small circle of friends over. They talked about Hebrews 13:5—Jesus promises never to leave us—and how the Holy Spirit fills the deepest loneliness with presence and peace. Emma began to understand that spiritual senses awaken through relationship—with God first, then with others.

5. Fear of Rejection and Not Measuring Up

When Emma feared rejection, her mom held her very close and reminded her of Psalm 139:14, "You are fearfully and wonderfully made." They started a gratitude journal to focus on God's blessings and strengths rather than fears. Her mom did model walking by faith, choosing to believe God's truth over the world's opinions, thereby encouraging

Emma to listen for the Holy Spirit's reassuring whispers at the moments of insecurity.

Both Parents Modeled:
- **Consistent Bible Engagement:** Reading Scripture wasn't a chore but a way to train spiritual senses to hear God's voice clearly.

- **Faith in Action:** They encouraged recognizing the Holy Spirit's gentle nudges—those "something told me..." moments—as real guidance.

- **Walking by Faith:** Choosing God's unseen reality over the loud, chaotic natural world, even when emotions or doubts try to convince otherwise.

Safe Spaces: Creating ongoing, grace-filled conversations where doubts and fears could be brought honestly, met with love, and guided back to God's truth. This type of very open dialogue will foster a sense of understanding and acceptance, making David and Emma feel truly heard and valued.

Teaching #3: A Mother's Conversation with Her Daughter: Understanding Temptation and Spiritual Awareness
Mom:

"Sweetheart, I want to talk to you today about something important to help you and that is temptation. You see, temptation isn't always loud or very obvious. Sometimes it's very quiet, sneaky, and very clever. It's like when someone tries to trick you without you even realizing it."

Daughter:
"How can temptation be sneaky, I don't get that? I had even thought that it was just about people asking me to do things that are wrong."

Mom:
"That is part of it, but there's more. Imagine a snake. You know how it moves silently and hides in the green grass? The enemy is a bit like that. In fact, when God's story about the beginning of the world was told, Satan chose the serpent because it's so subtle—so sneaky—that it can hide its true intentions. He wants you to focus on what you see around you—the people, the problems, the situations—so you won't see him coming."

Daughter:
"Why does he want to hide?"

Mom:
"Because if he was obvious, you could protect yourself. But by hiding behind situations or questions, he can confuse you. Like when he asked Eve, 'Did God really say...?' He wasn't just asking a question. He was trying to make her doubt what God had said to her and Adam in the garden, to make her question what was true. Temptation often starts with a question, not a command. It's very subtle, designed to make you second-guess God's words and promises."

Daughter:
"That sounds tricky. How do I know when I'm being tempted like that?"

Mom:
"Great question, you have asked. Temptation often comes dressed up as something harmless or even very good, but its real goal is to distract you from God. It makes you focus on what's around you or inside your head instead of on what God says. But remember how we talked about the Holy Spirit being like a SIM card in your phone? The Holy Spirit connects you to God's kingdom and helps you see beyond what's obvious."

Daughter:
"So the Holy Spirit helps me see the temptation coming?"

Mom:
"Yes! The Holy Spirit awakens your spiritual senses — like your inner spiritual eyes and ears. When you feel that little voice inside—sometimes it's very quiet, like a gentle warning saying, 'Be really careful,' or 'That's not right'—that's the Holy Spirit. He doesn't shout or force you. He's very gentle, like a whisper."

Daughter:
"But sometimes it's hard to listen. I might just think it's my imagination."

Mom:
"That happens a lot. Temptation loves it when you ignore that gentle whisper. But over time, as you get praying and spending time with God, your spiritual senses get stronger. You'll start to recognize those little nudges from the Holy Spirit which you did not know before now. And when you do, you'll have the strength to say 'no'—not because you're tough, but because you're connected to God's power."

Daughter:
"Like David, when he was worried about his exams and his dad prayed with him?"

Mom:
"Exactly. David learned to replace anxiety and fear with prayer and faith in God. The same goes for temptation. When you do feel pulled to do something wrong, pray. Ask the Holy Spirit to grant you grace, guide your thoughts and protect your heart. Remember, Satan is limited—he's not all-knowing or all-powerful. He does not know every thing, only God does. He needs you to give him information by doubting God's word or by ignoring the Spirit's warning."

Daughter:
"So, if I'm really connected to the Holy Spirit, I'm not alone in fighting temptation?"

Mom:
"Never alone. You have a helper inside of you. And just like the SIM card connects a real phone to a powerful network, the Holy Spirit connects you to God's power and wisdom.

You can walk by faith, trusting the unseen spiritual reality over what your natural eyes or mind might tell you. Temptation might try to trick you, but with God, you have the ultimate power to overcome."

Teaching #4: How to Replace Anxiety with Faith: A Mother-Daughter Conversation

Setting:
Emma, a 16-year-old high school student, who feels overwhelmed by her upcoming exams, social pressures, and her own future uncertainties. One very quiet evening, her mum notices Emma's restless pacing and her worried face.

Mom: "Hey, sweetie, you seem worried tonight. What is it? Want to talk about what's going on in your heart?"

Emma: (sighs) "I just can't stop thinking about exams, what my friends think of me, and what I'll even do after school. My chest feels very tight, and my mind won't stop racing."

Mom: "That sounds so hard, honey. You know, sometimes anxiety sneaks in when our mind starts taking thoughts too far—imagining worst-case scenarios that haven't even happened yet."

Emma: "Yeah, it feels like I'm stuck in a storm inside my head. What if I fail? What if I loose what is important to me? What if no one likes me? What if I mess up my future?"

Step 1: Recognising Anxiety Is Taking "Thought" Too Far
Mom explains: "Jesus said in Matthew 6:25, 28, and 31, 'Take no thought for your life.' That means don't let your mind carry worries so much that they weigh you down. Anxiety rides on 'need'—like when you think you *need* to be perfect or everyone *needs* to like you. When you focus only on what you *lack*, anxiety uses that crack in your armour to creep in."

Mom continues: "It's like when you imagine failing your exam, and suddenly you picture the shame, the disappointment, even the worst phone calls. Anxiety wants to trap you in fear so you feel helpless before the real fight even starts."

Step 2: Naming the Fear and Inviting Prayer
"Let's try something," Mom says gently. "When your mind floods with scary 'what ifs,' write them down or say them out loud. Then, instead of letting anxiety take you over, let those fears become a signal to pray."

Emma: "But what do I pray when I'm so scared?"

Mom: "You can say, 'God, I'm scared and overwhelmed, but I trust You to help me through this.' Philippians 4:6 reminds us to bring everything—our worries, needs, everything—to God in prayer. Prayer is like calling a lifeline. When you do, God doesn't always change the situation right away, but He changes *you*. He sends peace that protects your heart and mind like a shield."

Step 3: Experiencing God's Peace as a Protective Shield.
Emma closes her eyes, and Mom leads her softly: "Imagine your mind is a castle, and anxiety is trying to break down the gates with frightening thoughts. Now picture God's peace—a warm, glowing shield—covering your heart and mind, making those scary thoughts bounce off like raindrops."

Mom: "This peace is a special kind of calm that doesn't depend on your circumstances changing—it's a quiet strength inside you that keeps you safe from fear's attacks."

Step 4: Practising Daily Faith and Scripture
Mom shares: "Another teen I know, Sarah, used to panic before every test and social event. But she started of by reading verses like Psalm 139:14, 'I am fearfully and wonderfully made,' every morning. When anxiety came, she whispered those words and prayed until she felt God's peace like a calm river flowing through her."

Emma: "So, I can do that too? Like have my own 'peace shield'?"

Mom: "Exactly! And the more you read God's Word, the easier it becomes to hear His gentle voice—the one that says, 'You are not alone. I'm with you.'"

Step 5: Walking Through Anxiety Step-by-Step (Sarah's Story)
- **Sarah felt very anxious** about her schoolwork and future, often imagining that she would fail or disappoint her family.

- **Instead of fighting alone, she started praying**, telling God about every worry.

- She **chose one verse** (Philippians 4:6-7) and memorized it.

- When anxious thoughts came, she **paused, prayed**, and pictured God's peace guarding her mind.

- Slowly, Sarah noticed her **heart felt lighter**, and she could face challenges without the storm inside.

- Even when situations didn't immediately change, Sarah's **mind and soul were protected** by the peace God gave her.

Step 6: Leaving Fears Behind and Finding Tranquillity in God

Mom encourages Emma: "When the worries come back—and they will—remind yourself: *I am safe in God's hands.* Go to your 'worry box,' pray, read your favourite scripture, and breathe deeply, asking God to fill you with His peace."

Emma: "I think I can try that. It feels different imagining God's peace like a shield."

Mom: "And remember, prayer is a conversation, not a magic spell. Keep talking to God, even when it's really hard. Let His peace be the anchor for your soul, especially when your thoughts want to pull you under."

Summary:
- **Don't feed anxiety by overthinking 'what ifs.'**

- Turn worries into prayers.
- Claim God's peace as your protective shield.
- Use scripture to anchor your mind and heart.
- Practice daily faith like Sarah and Emma, and watch anxiety lose its hold and grip.

Teaching #5: A Mother's Hearty Conversation with Her Only Daughter: Discovering a New Realm with the Holy Spirit

Mom:

"Sweetheart, do you remember how we had talked about being born again earlier on? Jesus said, 'Except a man is born again, he cannot see the kingdom of God.' That means when you decide to follow Jesus, something amazing happens inside you — it's like being born into a completely new world."

Daughter:
"A new world? But I still see everything the same."

Mom:
"That's true — the world outside doesn't change right away. But inside your heart, a new reality begins to awaken. Imagine you're a phone. Before you put a SIM card in, your phone can do some things — like play music or take pictures — but the real power comes when you insert the SIM card. It connects you to the network, and suddenly you can call people, browse the internet, and do so much more."

Daughter:
"So, the Holy Spirit is like the SIM card?"

Mom:
"Exactly! When Jesus comes into your heart, the Holy Spirit is that like a SIM card. He connects you to God's kingdom — a spiritual realm that's real but invisible to your natural eyes. This connection opens your spiritual senses — your ability to hear, see, and feel God's presence in ways you couldn't before."

Daughter:
"But how do I know when I'm sensing God and not just my own thoughts?"

Mom:
"That's a great question. Think about a baby inside the womb — the baby has eyes and ears, but they don't really work until after birth. Your spiritual senses were there all along but asleep. Now, with the Holy Spirit inside you, they're waking up. It takes time and practice to trust them because God's voice is usually gentle — more like a quiet nudge than a loud shout."

Mom (continuing):
"You know, when we face danger or emergencies, sometimes our minds freeze — it's like everything shuts down. But your heart remains alive and alert. That's important because your heart is the tarmac where the Holy Spirit lands. If you have hidden his word in your heart, then

the Holy Spirit has a clear place to come down and guide you in the tough moments."

Daughter:
"So are you saying that, the Holy Spirit can't help me if my heart is closed off?"

Mom:
"Not fully. When your heart is open and honest, the Spirit can pull out courage, peace, and wisdom right when you need them most. But if your heart is cluttered or hiding things, it's harder to hear His voice or feel His peace. That's why it's so important to keep your heart very soft, to be able to talk openly with God and with people you do trust."

Example: How David Overcame Anxiety with His Father's Help

David was a teenager who felt anxious about exams and the future. His dad noticed and didn't just give advice — he sat with David one night and prayed together, asking the Holy Spirit to bring peace.

Dad:
"David, anxiety is like your mind trying to take control without God's help. Jesus said, 'Take no thought for your life.' That means don't carry your worries alone — bring them to God."

Together they read Jeremiah 29:11: *"For I know the plans I have for you," declares the Lord, "plans to prosper you and not to harm you, plans to give you hope and a future."* They talked about how David's worth wasn't in grades or approval but in God's love.

David learned to replace his racing thoughts with much prayers, and when anxiety hit, he would pause, pray, and listen for God's quiet peace — a peace that felt like a shield around his heart, protecting him from fear.

Walking by Faith: The New Realm vs. Natural Senses

Mom:
"Remember, the world around you is only part of a reality — the physical part. The spiritual realm is real but often unseen, like the wind. You can't see it, but you can feel it. When your spiritual senses are awaken, you begin to 'see' and 'hear' God's kingdom in new ways. It's a choice to live by faith — to trust what your spirit knows and gives to you even if your eyes can't yet see it."

Daughter:
"That sounds hard. How do I keep believing when I can't see it?"

Mom:
"It's like finding something precious hidden inside something ordinary — like when you pick up a tissue and find your mum's gold earring inside. Your heart recognizes the treasure before your mind even understands. Faith comes from your heart, where the Holy Spirit lives. Doubt tries to confuse your mind, but when you pray, ask God to open your spiritual eyes. He will."

Step-by-Step Guide to Replace Anxiety with Faith (Teen Example)

1. **Recognize anxiety:** Understand anxiety is your mind trying to take control without God's presence.

2. **Bring your worries to God in prayer:** *Philippians 4:6* says, "Be anxious for nothing, but in everything by prayer let your requests be made known to God."

3. **Listen for God's peace:** After praying, wait and sense the calm God places in your heart — a peace that guards you like a shield.

4. **Use Scripture as your shield:** Memorize verses like Jeremiah 29:11 and Psalm 139 to remind yourself of God's love.

5. **Practice spiritual awareness:** Notice gentle nudges from the Holy Spirit — those "something told me" moments — and trust them.

6. **Replace fear with faith:** When fear creeps back, respond with prayer, faith, and God's Word.

7. **Create safe spaces:** Talk openly with parents or trusted adults about doubts and fears — don't hide them.

A Final Encouragement

Mom:
"You're learning to live in two worlds — the physical and the spiritual. The Holy Spirit is your guide and protector. He teaches you to hear God's voice and keeps your heart peaceful even when the world is confusing. Faith isn't about seeing to believe — it's believing to see. And I'm here, walking this journey with you every step of the way."

Fathers Teaching 6#: Father's Teaching: Why Baptism Matters—Especially for Teens

"Dad, can I be baptized?"
This question came from my son's friend, Harry, after hearing a simple, powerful explanation I once shared with my son Nathan.

Let me tell you what I told them both—because if you're a teenager wondering about baptism, or a parent wondering if your teen is ready, this could change everything.

1. What Is Baptism Really About?
Many people think baptism is just a religious ritual—or something you do when you're older, like a spiritual graduation ceremony. But that's not how Scripture presents it.

Baptism is significant. Deeply significant.
Let's start with **Mark 16:16**:

"Whoever believes and is baptized will be saved, but whoever does not believe will be condemned."

Notice the order: *believe*, then *baptized*.

This shows us that **baptism is not for infants or unbelievers**. You cannot be baptized before salvation. you can only do it when you have decided to follow Jesus. It's a response to personal faith, not a substitute for it.

2. Two Kinds of Salvation: From Eternal Death and From the World

Let's go deeper.

Romans 10:9-10 says:

"If you declare with your mouth, 'Jesus is Lord,' and believe in your heart that God raised Him from the dead, you will be saved."

This kind of salvation is about **eternity**—being rescued from eternal separation from God. This happens **the moment you believe and confess faith in Christ.** No water needed.

But there's another layer of salvation that many do overlook.

You see, salvation isn't just about the afterlife. **It's also about freedom in this life.**

Think back to the Israelites in Egypt.

- **They were saved from death** the night of the Passover when they applied the blood of the lamb.

- But **Pharaoh still had power over them**.

- It wasn't until they **crossed the Red Sea**—a symbol of water baptism—that the *system of Egypt* lost its grip for good.

That's the second layer of salvation.

Not from **death**, but from **dominion**—from the system of the world that still tries to control you, tempt you, and keep you in cycles of fear, bondage, or confusion.

3. What Baptism Does in a Teen's Life

This is what I told Nathan one night as we read the Word together.

"Son, when you believe in Jesus, you're saved from eternal death. But when you're baptized, the devil knows you no longer belong to his system. It's like you're announcing to every spirit and power, 'I belong to Jesus now—body, soul, and spirit.'"

He shared this with his friend Harry, and Harry couldn't get it out of his head. A few days later, he came to us and said, "I want to be baptized. I believe in Jesus. I want that freedom, too."

We talked with his parents, and they agreed. He had already confessed faith in Christ—he understood the gospel, and now he wanted to seal that decision with water baptism.

4. Harry's Story: What Happened After His Baptism

Harry was baptized by full immersion—just like Jesus was.

And something happened that day.

He said later, "When I came out of the water, I felt like I left something behind in it. Like all the spiritual baggage I didn't even know I was carrying just fell off. It was like hell whispered, 'This one is Baptist. He no longer belongs to us.'"

That's the power of water baptism.

Not magic. Not religion.

Just **obedience and faith**—and heaven backs it up.

5. So, Can a Teenager Be Baptized?

The answer is **YES**—absolutely. But with this condition:

Only if they have personally believed in Jesus and confessed Him as Lord.

There is no "minimum age" in Scripture—but there *is* a requirement of personal **faith** and **understanding**. Baptism isn't a family tradition. It's a personal covenant.

It must be:

- **After salvation**
- **By full immersion** (not sprinkling)
- **A conscious decision** based on personal faith—not done to you as a baby

If your teen has confessed Christ, they are ready to take this next step. Baptism isn't a reward for spiritual maturity—it's the next step after believing.

6. Why It Matters for Parents and Teens

As a father, I don't want to just raise a moral kid—I want to raise a **free** one.

Free from fear. Free from addiction. Free from confusion. Free from the world's control.

And water baptism is one of the most powerful declarations of that freedom.

It's saying:

"I don't belong to Egypt anymore as one goes into water. I don't belong to the system of fear, sin, and confusion. I've crossed over and I'm now under Jesus' authority, one comes out of the water publicly."

Final Thoughts for Parents and Teens

To the Teen:
If you've believed in Jesus but haven't been baptized, don't wait. It's not about age—it's about ownership. You can belong to Jesus and still be harassed by the world until you make a public stand.

To the Parent:
Help your teen understand the weight and beauty of baptism. Not as pressure, but as invitation. Talk to them like I talked to Nathan. Be ready for the moment they say, "I'm ready."

And when they do?

Celebrate. Heaven is.

Father's Teaching 7# : The Inner Warning — Helping Teens Listen to God's Prompting

Father:
Hey son, can we talk for a few minutes today? There's something I wish I had learned earlier in life. It would have saved me a lot of pain if I had know it earlier. And I think it would very much help you too.

Son:
Sure, Dad. What's up?

Father:
It's about something I've come to call the *inner witness*—that quiet, uncomfortable feeling you get when something just doesn't sit right. It's not always loud or dramatic. Sometimes it's just a quiet check, like a very small alarm in your spirit. And if you do ignore it, you can end up doing things you are most likely will regret.

Let me explain it like this.

You know how sometimes, before you make a decision—especially when you're tempted to do something wrong—you feel a little uneasy, but then your mind starts trying to justify it?

Son:
Yeah... like when I know I probably shouldn't go along with something, but I start thinking, "It's not that bad."

Father:
Exactly. That's the battle. The Bible says in **1 John 2:26** that deception doesn't just jump on a child of God by surprise. Whenever a believer walks into deception, it's because they ignored the prompting of the Spirit. The peace you had goes away, and discomfort sets in. That's the warning.

But here's what happens—*you start arguing with it*. Your mind says, "Come on, it's not that serious," or "Everyone else is doing it," and that's what gets you in trouble. But if you learn to obey that initial discomfort—*before the argument wins*—you'll avoid so many traps.

Even if you don't have facts, even if nothing *looks* wrong, if your spirit is not at peace, listen to that.

Son:
So what do I do when that happens?

Father:
You say this to yourself:

"I don't have peace about this. I may not know why. But because I'm not comfortable doing this, I'm not going to do it."

That one decision can protect your life.

Let me give you two examples of two girls, Debby and Lydia—real girls, just like your classmates.

Debby's Choice: Listening to the Prompting

One day, Debby was invited to the park after school by a classmate. It seemed innocent, just two friends hanging out. But as she paused and checked in with her spirit—she felt that small, childlike warning. It was subtle, but strong enough to stop her. Then she heard a word in her spirit: **"Thief."**

That may sound strange—but instantly, she remembered **John 10:1**, where Jesus talks about the thief who comes to steal, kill, and destroy. She thought, *"Why would my classmate be a thief?"* She didn't have all the facts, but that warning was enough.

So she stayed home. Later, it came out that the classmate had planned to shoplift and drag her into it. Debby was spared—not because she was smart, but because she *listened*. She didn't joke with the prompting.

Son:
So if she had gone, she would've been in big trouble—even if she didn't do anything wrong herself?

Father:
Exactly. It's the association that could have cost her, her record, her peace, even her future. But she trusted that small voice. She walked in the light.

Now compare that with Lydia.

Lydia's Mistake: Light Will Still Find You

Lydia also had a friend who seemed trustworthy. She didn't feel any warning initially and went along with a plan that later turned out to be an attempt to commit fraud. The friend convinced her they needed to make money and this was a shortcut. Lydia trusted her. She didn't sense any deception at first.

But here's the grace of God—Lydia was still walking in the light. She still had a habit of reading her Bible and spending time with God. And during her quiet time at home, the Holy Spirit exposed the mistake. As she read the Word, that moment she compromised *lit up*—like a flashlight shining on dirt. Her spirit was convicted. She saw clearly where she had been deceived.

That's **1 John 1:5–7** in action:

"If we walk in the light... the blood of Jesus cleanses us from all sin."

Even though she messed up, because she was still in fellowship with God, the truth came. She wasn't abandoned.

Son:
So are you saying that even when I make a mistake, if I'm walking with God, and that He'll bring me back?

Father:
Yes. That's what I want you to understand. **God doesn't abandon us.** He is *jealous* for His children. Even if you start to wander off, His jealousy will bring you back.

But here's the key: **don't joke with the prompting**. It may come like a small nudge, or a quiet warning, or even just a sudden loss of peace. Respect that. Obey that. *It will preserve you.*

Let me also say this clearly—**God is not judging you for Adam's sin.** Romans 6:23 says:

"The wages of *sin* is death."

That means it's our **own** sin, our personal rebellion, that will be judged—not what Adam did. You're not guilty because of Adam's own sin which he commited by disobeying God's command. You're responsible for your own choices. And that's why it's so important to walk in the Spirit and stay sensitive to His guidance.

Son:
That's a lot to think about. I've definitely felt that unease before. Sometimes I ignored it. But I get now why I shouldn't.

Father:
It cost me a lot when I didn't listen to that witness, son. I ignored it many times, thinking I knew better. But now, I know better. So I'm passing this on to you—don't joke with the gentle presence of the Spirit. It's not just your conscience. It's God Himself keeping you from harm.

You might not always understand why. You might not even have a reason. But that inner "no" is enough. Trust it. It will keep you from harm—even from what you can't see yet.

To Parents: How to Help Your Teen Listen to the Spirit
1. **Teach them to recognize the inner witness.**

2. It's not about fear or guilt—it's about peace or the loss of it. Help your teen understand that this is God's way of speaking before things go wrong.

3. **Affirm that they are responsible for their own choices.**

4. Teens must understand that it's not Adam's sin they'll be judged for—it's their own. This empowers them to take responsibility and walk wisely.

5. **Encourage them to follow the "no peace, no action" principle.**

6. Even without full information, train them to pause if peace is missing.

7. **Keep them in fellowship with the Word.**

8. Like Lydia, even when mistakes happen, staying in the Word brings correction and restoration. God's light always reveals what's hidden.

9. **Model your own obedience.**

10. Share your mistakes. Let them know you didn't always get it right—and what it cost you. Your transparency builds trust and makes your teaching real.

Father's Final Words to Son:

Stay in the light, son. God's jealousy will preserve you if your heart desires the real truth. Even when you mess up, He'll pull you back. But the safest, wisest thing you can do is this: trust the witness. That quiet "no" may one day save your life.

Conclusion:
Raising Teens with a Legacy of Wisdom

Parenting teenagers is less a sprint and more a marathon—a marathon of faith, grace, and showing up day after day, even when it's hard. You don't have to be perfect. Nobody is. What matters most is faithfulness: the simple, steady commitment to love your teen unconditionally and point them toward Jesus, no matter what.

It's easy to feel overwhelmed or question if you're "doing enough." Maybe you've doubted your very self, lost patience, or wished for more precise answers. That's normal. Remember, parenting isn't about having all the right words or perfect plans—it's about being present, willing to walk alongside your teen through every mess and miracle.

Remember, your teen's future isn't just about the decisions they make today.. It's about who they become at their core—their identity in Christ. And God's Spirit is already at work, gently awakening their hearts, even in moments when you can't see it. Trust that divine work. Trust that His plans for your child are good, full of hope and a future (Jeremiah 29:11).

Hold onto these truths when the road gets tough:

- **Rejection is not their identity—God's unchanging love is.** Your teen may face "no's" and hard knocks, but they are infinitely valued by the One who made them.

- **Remember, hard seasons aren't punishment—they're rather preparation.** Every challenge they endure is shaping resilience, character, and a deeper faith. These are the building blocks of a strong, wise, and secure future for your teen. **Keep in mind, faith means trusting what you can't see, even when fears screams. Your** journey of faith embodies this truth in real life, serving as a powerful example for your teen. A visual aid. **Wise choices emerge from a heart that is rooted in God's Word and a daily pursuit of Him.** Encourage your teen to build that foundation, and you'll see the fruit over time.

You are not alone in this. Every parent experiences moments of doubt and exhaustion, as well as moments of joy and breakthrough. Your commitment to loving your teen through it all is building something eternal—a legacy of wisdom and grace that will outlast every fleeting trend, challenge, and mistake.

Keep walking this journey by faith, day by day, moment by moment. You are raising not just teenagers but future men and women of God—very strong, wise, and secure in a world that often feels uncertain.

A Prayer for Parents and Teens

Holy Spirit, wake up our spiritual senses. Help us hear Your voice above all others. Teach us to walk by faith, to know our identity in You, and to make wise choices every day. Give parents patience and strength to love well, and teens courage to trust You in every storm. Remind us all that Your love never fails and Your grace is enough. Amen.

Please Leave a Review!

I would be incredibly thankful if you could take just 60 seconds to write a brief review on the platform of purchase, even if it's just a few sentences!

Other Books You'll Love!

---

1. <u>The Fear of The Lord: How God's Honour Guarantees Your Peace</u>

2. Parenting Teenage Girls for Purpose: Guiding Godly Young Girls to Walk in Charisma, Character, Calling, Life Skills, and Christ-Centered Confidence

3. Parenting Teenage Boys for Purpose: Guiding Godly Young Girls to Walk in Charisma, Character, Calling, Life Skills, and Christ-Centered Confidence

4. <u>Raising Teenagers to Choose Wisely: Keeping your Teen Secure in a Big World</u>

5. <u>Spelling one: An Interactive Vocabulary & Spelling Workbook for 5-Year-Olds. *(With Audiobook Lessons)*</u>

6. <u>Spelling Two: An Interactive Vocabulary & Spelling Workbook for 6-Year-Olds. *(With Audiobook Lessons)*</u>

7. <u>Spelling Three: An Interactive Vocabulary & Spelling Workbook for 7-Year-Olds. *(With Audiobook Lessons)*</u>

8. <u>Spelling Four: An Interactive Vocabulary & Spelling Workbook for 8-Year-Olds.</u> *(With Audiobook Lessons)*

9. <u>Spelling Five: An Interactive Vocabulary & Spelling Workbook for 9-Year-Olds.</u> *(With Audiobook Lessons)*

10. <u>Spelling Six: An Interactive Vocabulary & Spelling Workbook for 10 & 11 Years Old.</u> *(With Audiobook Lessons)*

11. <u>Spelling Seven: An Interactive Vocabulary & Spelling Workbook for 12-14 Years-Old.</u> *(With Audiobook Lessons)*

12. <u>Raising Boys in Today's Digital World: Proven Positive Parenting Tips for Raising Respectful, Successful, and Confident Boys</u>

13. <u>Raising Girls in Today's Digital World: Proven Positive Parenting Tips for Raising Respectful, Successful, and Confident Girls</u>

14. <u>Raising Kids in Today's Digital World: Proven Positive Parenting Tips for Raising Respectful, Successful, and Confident Kids</u>

15. <u>The Child Development and Positive Parenting Master Class 2-in-1 Bundle: Proven Methods for Raising Well-Behaved and Intelligent Children, with Accelerated Learning Methods</u>

16. Parenting Teens in Today's Challenging World 2-in-1 Bundle: Proven Methods for Improving Teenager's Behaviour with Positive Parenting and Family Communication

17. Life Strategies for Teenagers: Positive Parenting, Tips and Understanding Teens for Better Communication and a Happy Family

18. Parenting Teen Girls in Today's Challenging World: Proven Methods for Improving Teenager's Behaviour with Whole Brain Training

19. Parenting Teen Boys in Today's Challenging World: Proven Methods for Improving Teenager's Behaviour with Whole Brain Training

20. 101 Tips For Helping With Your Child's Learning: Proven Strategies for Accelerated Learning and Raising Smart Children Using Positive Parenting Skills

21. 101 Tips for Child Development: Proven Methods for Raising Children and Improving Kids Behavior with Whole Brain Training

22. Financial Tips to Help Kids: Proven Methods for Teaching Kids Money Management and Financial Responsibility

23. Healthy Habits for Kids: Positive Parenting Tips for Fun Kids Exercises, Healthy Snacks, and Improved Kids Nutrition

24. Mini Habits for Happy Kids: Proven Parenting Tips for Positive Discipline and Improving Kids' Behavior

25. Good Habits for Healthy Kids 2-in-1 Combo Pack: Proven Positive Parenting Tips for Improving Kid's Fitness and Children's Behavior

26. T Raising Teenagers to Choose Wisely: Keeping your Teen Secure in a Big World

27. Tips for #CollegeLife: Powerful College Advice for Excelling as a College Freshman

28. The Career Success Formula: Proven Career Development Advice and Finding Rewarding Employment for Young Adults and College Graduates

29. The Motivated Young Adult's Guide to Career Success and Adulthood: Proven Tips for Becoming a Mature Adult, Starting a Rewarding Career, and Finding Life Balance

30. Bedtime Stories for Kids: Short Funny Stories and poems Collection for Children and Toddlers

31. Guide for Boarding School Life

Facebook Community

I will like to invite you to our Facebook community group to visit this link and simply click the join group.

https://www.facebook.com/profile.php?id=61563572125960

This is a private group where parents, teachers, and carers can learn, share tips, ask questions, discuss and get valuable content about raising and parent modern children. It is a very supportive and encouraging group where valuable content, free resources, and exciting discussion about parenting are being shared. You can use this to benefit from social media. You will be learning a lot from school teachers, experts, counselors, new and experienced parents, and stay updated with our latest releases.

See you there!

Your Free Gift!

As a way of saying thank you for Your purchase, I have included a gift that you can download at <u>TCEC publishing .com</u>

References

[1] https://cchp.ucsf.edu/sites/g/files/tkssra181/f/SelfEsteem_en0710.pdf

[2] https://www.theseus.fi/bitstream/handle/10024/50239/Anttila_Marianna_Saikkonen_Pinja.pdf

[3] https://ijcat.com/archives/volume5/issue2/ijcatr05021006.pdf

[4] https://www.harvey.k-state.edu/family-and-consumer-sciences/family_and_child_development/documents/CommunicatingwTeenTrust.pdf

[5] https://www.researchgate.net/publication/283721084_Early_Reading_Development

[6] https://www.understood.org/en/friends-feelings/empowering-your-child/building-on-strengths/download-hands-on-activity-to-identify-your-childs-strengths

[7] https://www.wfm.noaa.gov/pdfs/ParentingYourTeen_Handout1.pdf

[8] https://www.helpguide.org/articles/depression/parents-guide-to-teen-depression.htm?pdf=13027

[9] https://www2.ed.gov/parents/academic/help/adolescence/adolescence.pdf

[10] http://centerforchildwelfare.org/kb/prprouthome/Helping%20Your%20Children%20Navigate%20Their%20Teenage%20Years.pdf

[11] https://www.childrensmn.org/images/family_resource_pdf/027121.pdf

[12] https://educationnorthwest.org/sites/default/files/developing-empathy-in-children-and-youth.pdf

[13] http://drkateaubrey.com/wp-content/uploads/2016/02/Parenting-Your-Strong-Willed-Child.pdf

[14] https://www.researchgate.net/publication/263227023_Family_Time_Activities_and_Adolescents'_Emotional_Well-being

[15] https://parenting-ed.org/wp-content/themes/parenting-ed/files/handouts/communication-parent-to-child.pdf

[16] https://www.wikihow.mom/Trust-Your-Teenager

[17] https://www.statmodel.com/download/Meeus,%20vd%20Schoot,%20Klimstra%20&.pdf

[18] https://www.nap.edu/resource/19401/ProfKnowCompFINAL.pdf

[19] http://www.delmarlearning.com/companions/content/1418019224/AdditionalSupport/box11.1.pdf

[20] http://resources.beyondblue.org.au/prism/file?token=BL/1810_A

[21] https://exeter.anglican.org/wp-content/uploads/2014/11/Listening-to-children-leaflet_NCB.pdf

[22] https://www.researchgate.net/publication/312600262_Creative_Thinking_among_Preschool_Children

[23] https://www.gutenberg.org/files/15114/15114-pdf.pdf

[24] https://discovery.ucl.ac.uk/id/eprint/1522668/1/Thesis%20Moulton%20V%20281016.pdf

[25] https://www.bda.uk.com/foodfacts/healthyeatingchildren.pdf

[26] http://www.tuskmont.org/uploads/1/7/7/2/17728377/follow_the_child_trust_the_child.pdf

[27] https://www.apa.org/pi/families/resources/develop.pdf

www.ingramcontent.com/pod-product-compliance
Lightning Source LLC
Chambersburg PA
CBHW052034070526
44584CB00016B/2032